JN437629

LETS (Let's learn English Through Sport) WRITING!

Joe Trolan Ph.D Candidate
& Seong-Hee Park Ph.D

HU:iNE

Contents

Introduction

Sport and the sport industry have had a tremendous impact on modern society; the subject 'sport' has become our daily topic due to its global and popular nature for everyone.

Just like the two major characteristics 'global' and 'popular', sport have played critical roles in our society, knowing, getting familiar with, and using English in our daily life has become a natural phenomenon anywhere in the world. Therefore, it comes as no surprise that sport and English have something special in common.

This book is designed to help the ESL student understand and learn how to write English through sport. With this book, students will have the opportunity to understand the various stages of English writing from pre-writing, paragraph formats, to essay formats. In addition, they will have the opportunity to practice and discuss their writing with their classmates with critical articles on the sport industry.

Because of commonalities between sport and English, you do not have to have played any sport to be able to use this book. All you need is to become interested in sport or sport-related subject. Are you interested in sport? Then, we are sure that you are ready for the book.

Let's learn English writing with this book. Do not worry and just jump over the fence of English writing. Just do it now as Michal Jordan jumped over his opponents with the legendary slogan in the sport industry: Just Do It!

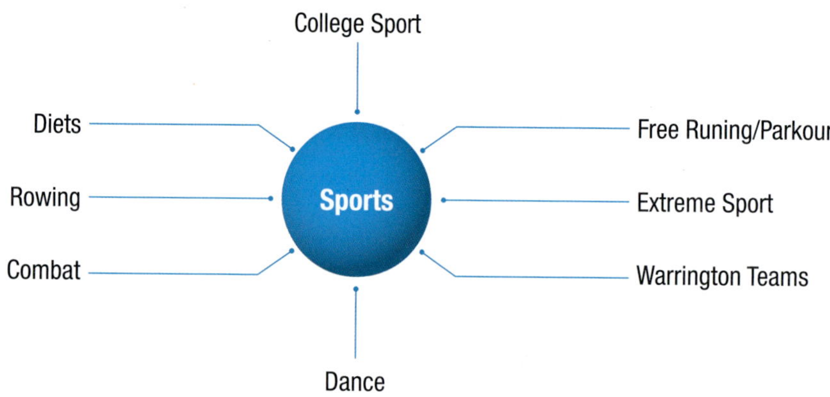

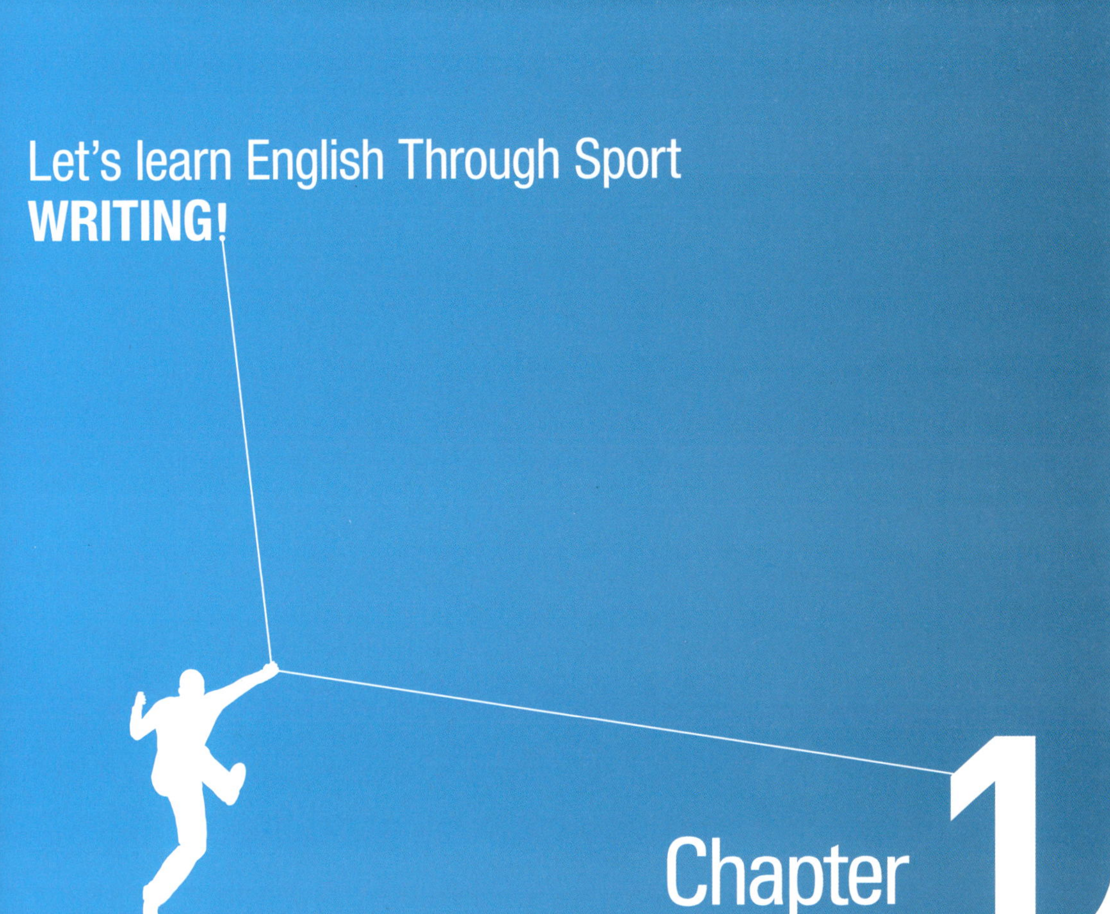

Chapter 1

The basics of the writing process?

Chapter 1

The basics of the writing process

In this Chapter

In this unit the reader will learn about the steps in the writing process and how to utilize these to eventually form an overall understanding of how to write an academic essay. We will also discuss common problems that students should be aware of as second language learners

1. The writing process

A. The writing process is not complicated but is often times misused as people tend to bypass certain steps because of various reasons. It is important for English second language learners to understand and learn the importance of all the steps. Bypassing steps can lead to a poorly written or thought out paper and will only increase the time and stress involved in writing the paper.

2. The following steps are considered the relevant steps of the writing process.

A. Step One: Choose a topic

1) This step is important because if you choose a topic that you are not familiar with or do not understand then you may have trouble forming ideas or gathering information. Therefore, at the beginning of your writing class, the student should choose topics that they are familiar with such as favorite sport teams, favorite sports, or favorite athletes.

2) For Example, you could choose a topic on one of the following

- Greatest Sports team

- Greatest Sport Athlete

- Craziest sport you have ever watched.

B. Step Two: Idea Gathering

1) Once you have decided on your topic, then you want to write as many ideas as you can about your topic. This stage does not have to be grammatically correct or structured; the student should get as many ideas as possible down on paper. The student can do this through various techniques that will be explained later in this book such as brainstorming.

2) For Example, if you choose the greatest sports team, you could research what have been the most successful teams. It could be the Brazilian national soccer team, the Los Angeles Lakers, the Dallas Cowboys, or Liverpool football club.

C. Step Three: Organize

1) This step involves the student examining all of his or hers ideas that they gathered in Step B and decide which of them are the most relevant for their paper. The student can create a map of ideas that shows when and where to use the ideas.

D. Step Four: Write

1) In this step the student after gathering and organizing their ideas begins to write the paragraph or paper. It is ok for the student to refer the notes about the ideas and how to organize the paper.

E. Step Five: Review

1) This step involves reviewing what you have just written. This is an important step because without this step the student can miss mistakes or areas that could be improved on. Therefore, the student should use this step to add more information if necessary and remove unnecessary information. Additionally, the student should read their papers or have a friend read their paper for any errors. Having another person analysis your paper can help your writing techniques and the students understanding of how to write.

F. Step Six: Revise and Rewrite

1) This step requires the student to revise what they wrote in the previous step. The student may again add or subtract from their paper or even reorganize parts of the paper or paragraph. The student should fully proofread their paper and have a friend proofread the paper for errors. If errors are found they should be fixed and then your paper or

paragraph is finished.

3. Common Problems

A. Capitalization

1) One of the major concerns with writers of English as a second language is the use of capitalized words. At the beginning of every sentence you should us a capitalized letter. For example –the ball went out of play after Eointook a shot.The writer should us a capital "T" at the beginning –The ball went out of play after Eoin took a shot.

2) Additionally, the names of people should be capitalized

- Kim, Se-Yun
- Steven Gerrard
- George Best

3) Use the correct capitalization for the following names

- kevinkeegan
- neillennon
- John aldridge

4) The names of cities, countries, and continents are also capitalized. Also, days, months,

seasons, and place names are capitalized

- Africa, Asia, and Europe
- Belgium, France, Korea, and Spain
- Seoul, Tokyo, Belfast, and London

5) Use the correct capitalization for the following:

- paris
- rome
- daegu

B. Period

1) Punctuation is also very important and the writer should put a period at the end of every sentence or command.

- Jimmy kicked the ball.
- Give me the ball.

2) Write a similar sentence with correct periods

-

-

-

3) Question marks (?) should be placed at the end of all questions

- Did you have fun today at the game?

- What was the score of the game today?

4) Write a similar sentence with correct question marks

-

-

-

C. Sentence structure

1) Line management– one of the problems encountered is students using a new line for each sentence. Sentences do not need to be on a new line but as a continuation on the same line

2) For example: Poor line management.

- The score of today's game was 1-0.

- Sean Sweeney scored the goal.

- It was a really good game.
  → There is no need for 3 lines for these sentences

3) Example of correct line management

- The score of today's game was 1-0. Sean Sweeney scored the goal and it was a really great game

4. Key questions

A. Where to start

1) The toughest question is where to start– a student should follow the steps and this will help them develop ideas and topics for papers

B. How to start

1) The student by following the steps will develop ideas on his/her topic and these ideas can be organized into a paper structure. This will be developed more in the upcoming chapters.

5. Words to know

A. Steps Paragraph Gather

Organize	Essay	Proofread
Review	Rewrite	Topic

6. Questions about the reading

Reporting troublemakers just a text away

Unruly fans

Some fans' applause during the Miami Heat's recent home opener had nothing to do with a Dwyane Wade breakaway dunk against the New York Knicks.

Instead, several ticket holders in the lower bowl clapped after security officials ejected a verbally abusive patron from AmericanAirlines Arena. The action came after a concerned customer sitting near the troublemaker sent a text message to building management, alerting them of the problem.

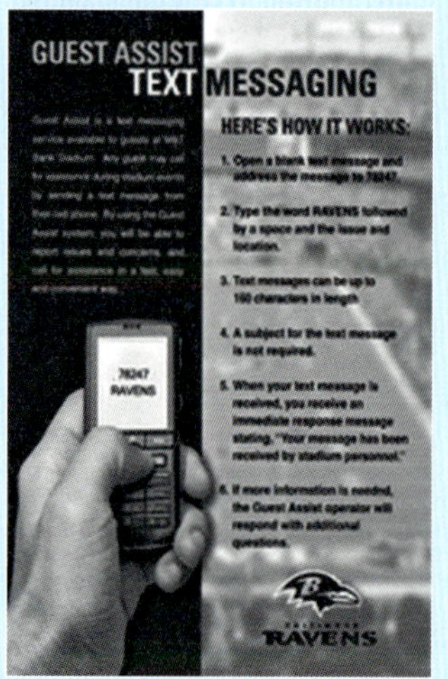

The Baltimore Ravens report a lukewarm response to texting among their fans.

The use of texting is a convenient and anonymous form of communication to quickly inform sports facility operators of an issue requiring their attention, whether it's a beverage spill, broken seat or a foul-mouthed fan.

The benefit of texting for teams and crowd management firms is that fans can alert facility operators to an issue in the stands without leaving their seats to find an usher, guest services or a security worker.

In Miami, for example, fans text the word "heat," the issue and seating location to a specific number. The text is sent to the arena's command center and an administrator's pager. That person is assigned to confirm the message and respond to the issue, said Kim Stone, the arena's executive vice president and general manager.

Every NFL stadium now has a text message system in place, and several MLB parks have tapped into the programs provided by vendors such as GuestAssist and In Stadium Solutions. Vendors are developing newer technology that can further integrate texting into a building's incident management software system.

NBA and NHL arenas using texting include AmericanAirlines Arena, American Airlines Center in Dallas, Pepsi Center in Denver, Scottrade Center in St. Louis and Wachovia Center in Philadelphia.

Stickers remind fans about the text messaging system in place at Philadelphia Eagles games.

Stone said the Heat uses texting to empower fans to report incidents such as the "aggressive trash talking" that occurred during the home opener.

"Everyone has a different tolerance level for behavior," she said. "This system allows each person to reach us discreetly so we can address it when they find someone else's actions offensive."

In addition, the text message program provides additional eyes and ears to assist crowd managers stationed in seating sections. "Security can't be everywhere, and before an issue becomes a fight, we have to nip it in the bud," Stone said. "Texting is another means of becoming more proactive and allows us to address it before it escalates into something worse."

Texting doesn't work everywhere in sports, however. At M&T Bank Stadium in Baltimore, the Ravens encourage season-ticket holders to use their mobile devices to text their concerns. But for whatever reason, the team has not seen enough people tapping into the program to realize its full benefit, said Roy Sommerhof, vice president of stadium operations.

In Raleigh at RBC Center, which is run by the Carolina Hurricanes, arena officials tried a similar program on a limited basis last season before deciding it was not worth the trouble, said Larry Perkins, the arena's assistant general manager. Employees used the system more than hockey fans did to report incidents such as spills, and the building's command center received its fair share of prank texts, Perkins said.

Officials believe that mobile radios provide a quicker and more effective way to communicate and respond to a crowd management issue. Perkins summed up the team's philosophy for rejecting the technology: "Don't create a problem if there isn't one."

A. QUESTIONS

1) What is the writer trying to explain?

2) What ideas does he use to explain his message?

7. Writing assignment

A. Review and fill in the chart of what the steps contain

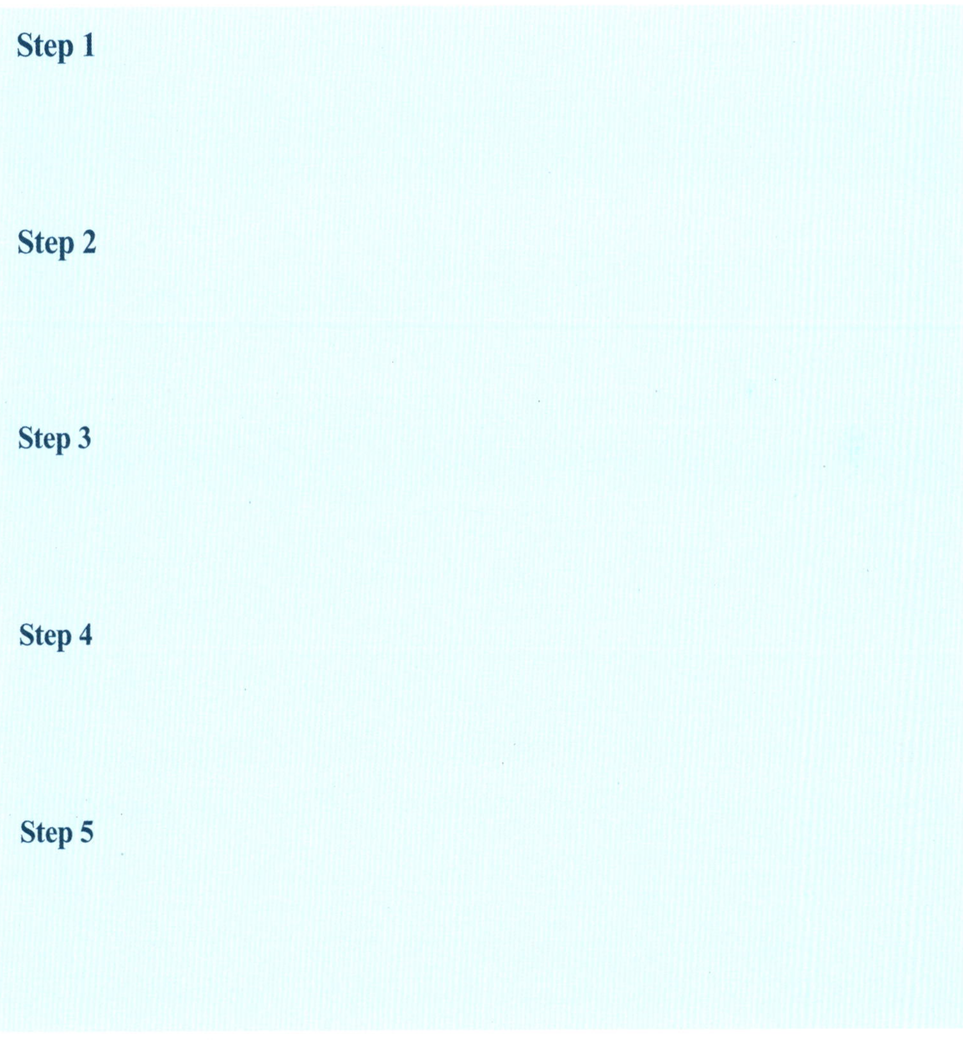

Step 6

B. Read the article and describe what the topic is

How to protect the exclusivity in your brand's sponsorship

Congratulations! You're the director of marketing for a major soft drink and you just signed an agreement to sponsor a professional sports team. Your agreement states that your brand is the team's exclusive soft drink sponsor and that no other soft drinks will be signed as team sponsors. Sounds like an airtight deal, right?

Not in today's world. For example, what if the team has a beer sponsor who later acquires a competing soft drink brand? Or what if a competing soft drink wants to sponsor the team's stadium (but not the team)? Or what if a competing soft drink wants to sponsor the brand-new online broadcasts of the team's games?

Issues such as these are becoming more common in today's sports sponsorship landscape. Failure to adequately address them up front may reduce the value of your brand's sponsorship, lead to conflicts between sponsors and teams or leagues, and result in potentially costly legal battles (as evidenced by the litigation between AT&T and NASCAR over competitive sponsorship issues).

In order to create a solid sponsorship agreement, parties need to recognize and address the likely issues and draft carefully for as many contingencies as possible, including defining competing brands and exclusivity.

■ **Who is a competitor?**

Defining vague or ambiguous terms is a classic challenge in contract drafting. This is especially true in today's world, where cell phones can double as Internet providers and banks offer everything from checking accounts to investment services. Thus, defining the competing brands in a sponsorship agreement can be trickier than ever. For example, is a product like flavored water competing with soft drinks? What about iced teas? Energy drinks? Defining competitor merely by using a category name is often unhelpful when categories can be so muddy. On the other hand, merely listing specific competitors fails to protect the sponsor if new competitors enter the market.

AT&T and NASCAR's disagreement is a good example of what can happen when exclusivity is not adequately addressed.

One solution to this definitional problem is to use a definition that is indexed to a third-party categorization system that updates as new brands enter the market. For instance, a soft drink sponsor might identify a categorization system used by the beverage industry. Defining "competitor" as any brand that falls into a certain category in that system would ensure that both parties understood exactly which brands were included as competitors up front while also ensuring that new brands entering the market would be covered as competitors.

In addition to carefully defining what a competitive sponsor is, your company may want to contract against a clashing sponsor, i.e., sponsors that are not competitive in the traditional sense but that might be embarrassing or otherwise counter to the goals of the existing sponsor. For instance, a candy bar sponsor might see its sponsorship value decrease if a weight loss company became a fellow sponsor. While certain clashing sponsors could be easily named in the sponsorship agreement, others might be hard to anticipate.

Finally, sponsorship agreements need to consider issues related to multifaceted companies and corporate mergers and acquisitions. For instance, if a noncompeting sponsor acquires or is acquired by a company that is competitive with your brand, your company needs to have provisions that minimize exposure of the competitive aspect of the other sponsor. Similarly, if a noncompeting sponsor has a subsidiary that is competitive with your brand, your sponsorship agreements need to be clear that only the noncompeting parent brand may be used in connection with the sponsorship. Details as specific as what logos and names may or may not be displayed should be spelled out in the agreement, as should details on how corporate name changes will be handled.

■ What is exclusive?

Even if a sponsorship agreement is clear on who competitors are, there is still the issue of which sponsorship activities are exclusive and which are open to competitors. For instance, a team may sell exclusive naming rights to its stadium but also wish to sell sponsorships for entrances, lounges or other sub-parts of the stadium. Similarly, a league that broadcasts games on two television networks may grant exclusive sponsorships to two competing brands from the same category, one on each channel. Sponsorship agreements need to clearly indicate in what areas a sponsor is being granted exclusive rights so as to avoid conflict.

Careful definition of exclusive areas of sponsorship inventory is particularly relevant these days given the proliferation of new media. Today's sports sponsorships can include exposure both on traditional media and new media as diverse as Web sites, online game broadcasts, mobile content, video games, simulations, YouTube, Twitter and more. Not only do these new media need to be addressed, but the agreement should also provide contingencies for unknown media that may be developed in the future.

As television ratings for sporting events decrease and commercials fall prey to digital recording technology, sports sponsorships will become increasingly important avenues to establish a company's brand. As sports entities increase their sponsorship inventory and sponsors race to secure exclusives, the potential for conflict between sponsors and teams will increase. Careful drafting of sponsorship agreements to address as many problems as possible can help ensure that the contracting parties maximize their benefit from their exclusive sponsorship while reducing potential conflict.

C. Match the words.

1) Paragraph •	• To arrange a clear plan
2) Gather •	• A paper that is 5 paragraphs long
3) Proofread •	• A group of related sentences
4) Steps •	• Idea of the paper
5) Essay •	• To collect information
6) Organize •	• To check for errors
7) Topic •	• A series of things to do

‹‹‹ MEMO ›››

‹‹‹ MEMO ›››

‹‹‹ MEMO ›››

‹‹‹ **MEMO** ›››

‹‹‹ **MEMO** ›››

Getting Started : The Pre-writing process

Chapter 2

Getting Started: The Pre-writing process

In this Chapter

You will learn how to choose and narrow a topic. How to map and brain storm a topic of interest and utilize techniques to encourage free writing.

The Pre-writing process

In our daily lives we frequently have writing assignments. From memos for things to do, to grocery lists, to emails, to thank you cards, or class work, we continually write everyday on topics. Each area of interest has different levels of writing formalities but there are several points that a student should keep in mind when planning to write.

‹‹‹ *Take out a scrap of paper and write about yourself. Discuss your childhood and what sports you played or were interested in. Then give this paper to a partner and ask your partner to describe the details of your topic – that would be you* ›››

1. The writing process

Before starting the writing process, the student must think about the topic or subject of the paper. Many times students draw a blank when thinking about a paper or struggle to develop a cohesive topic. This is because we are not prepared for writing and you are not alone. From the freshman to accredited authors, at times they have stared at blank screens or sheets of paper. How do we then overcome this problem? We can do so with strategies or techniques that can allow the student to plan what you are going to write.

A. Plan A: The steps

From the previous chapter we mentioned the steps of the writing process and this is the normal way to start writing. First, state your topic; second, write an outline; third, write the initial draft, fourth, read and rewrite. Of course this traditional way may not work so we must have a plan B.

B. Plan B: The Gather

This plan has several components and all can be used to help with the flow of ideas for your paper and will be discussed in greater detail in this chapter. One of the initial ways to gather information is to ask yourself about why you are writing the paper

1) Academic paper reason

2) Newspaper article reason

3) Email reason

4) Letter reason

As you can see there are many different reasons for writing – the question you should ask is "so what?" Do you want to inform, persuade, compare, or describe – each purpose can have a different writing strategy.

5) Example:

Give 3 reasons why you support your favorite team.

-

-

-

Give 3 reasons why you think soccer is an exciting or boring sport.

-

-

-

Give 3 reasons why you think Lionel Messi is a better soccer player than Cristiano Ronaldo

-

-

-

These reasons are the start of your ideas. They can help you describe your topic, help you describe why it's important and tell the reader a story – this is the idea of Brainstorming and Mapping. The first step though is to choose your topic

2. Choosing and narrowing your topic

A. How to choose your topic

This can be one of the most difficult stages in the writing process and one that can cause the writer a lot of anxiety or stress. Your topic is the idea for your paper or your paragraph and there are a few things that you should remember before your start to write – DO NOT SELECT A TOPIC THAT YOU ARE UNFAMILIAR WIITH.

1) Who is Pele

2) Who is Enda Morris

3) What is a traditional sport of Afghanistan

4) What is a traditional sport of your country

5) Which can you write more about????

‹‹‹ *Take out a piece of paper and write about your favorite television program and spend five minutes writing about it, then do the same for a famous Television program in the United Kingdom – which did you struggle with?* ›››

- First, choose a topic that is not to narrow or limited. When a topic is too limited there are not enough ideas to write about in your paper. The color of the uniforms of my team is too limited or narrow to write about.

- Second, choose a topic that is not to broad or very general. If a topic is broad then the author may have too many ideas and the paper can be too "busy."Remember each paragraph should have one idea – if topic is soccer, it is very general with hundreds of ideas. You want to narrow the topic

- Rather than just write about soccer, you could narrow the topic to:
  The English Premier league is better than the Spanish league
  Liverpool is the most successful English football club
  Brazil is the most successful nation at the world cup

B. Choose two topics from the following list and narrow each down to a potential paper topic. Then compare with a partner.

1) Athletes

2) Countries

3) Olympics

4) Youth Sport

5) Steroids

The next step in prewriting once you have chosen your topic is to gather information and ideas. This is called Brainstorming

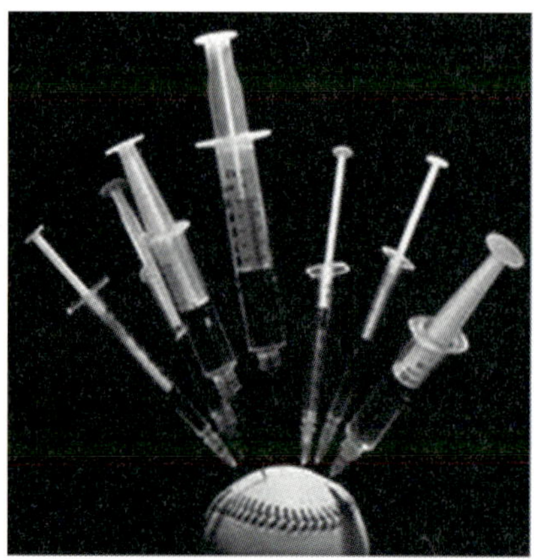

3. Brainstorming

A. What is brainstorming?

Brainstorming is part of the writing process that involves gathering ideas about your topic, or creating lists of for your topic. There are many ways to brainstorm but you should think of it as a heavy snow storm with lots of snowflakes. Once these snowflakes land they gather together to form snow. The same with your ideas – you want to write down as many ideas as you can think. These ideas can be fantastic or silly or extraneous– it doesn't matter, at this stage you want to write down as many ideas as possible.

1) Example – come up with some ideas for these topics and compare with your partner or class.

- Who is your favorite athlete and why

- What is your favorite sport and why

As you can see there are numerous ideas and there are several ways to brainstorm and we will examine listing, free-writing, and mapping.

B. Listing

Think of an earlier topic that we discussed and write single words or phrases that are connected to that topic. Here is an example of "why I think StevenGerrard is the greatest midfielder in the world

Making a list

V Liverpool player
V Great midfielder
V Loyal
V Passing the ball
V English
V Respected
V Controls the game
V Amazing vision

1) Working with a partner or on your own make a list with as many ideas for the following topics

- Successful Korean athletes abroad

- Kim Yuna advertising

- Athletes and military service

Now working from the list as many ideas as you can in 10 minutes

C. Free-writing

Free-writing is the act of writing whatever comes into your thoughts about your topic. There are no mistakes or stopping – it is just writing what is in your head. When you free-write you do not need to worry about having correct grammar or spelling –it's all about ideas. If you make a mistake just scratch out and keep going –

1) Example

> The reason why I think Steven Gerrard is the greatest midfielder is because he is an amazing passer of the ball ~~and runs all day~~. His vision is beyond that of any other players in the English Premier League and is probably the best in a generation. He has been extremely loyal and honest to Liverpool football club. He is greatly respected throughout the world by other soccer players ~~and will win the league one day~~.

B. Choose a topic and practice your free-writing for 10 minutes – remember DO NOT STOP or ERASE – just write as much as you can.

D. Mapping

The third type of brainstorming is the idea of mapping. This is a simple concept where the student uses a map to cluster ideas together. You first start by writing your topic in the middle of a sheet of paper with a circle around it. Then add more circles around your topic circle and connect with lines to show that they are connected. These secondary circles are your supporting ideas, you can then add more circles to either the secondary or primary circles as you

see fit. The following example i s a map of "why I think the EPL is the greatest league in the world." The student had four secondary ideas which were best players, most oversea fans, television, and excitement. The student the connected most overseas with Asia and America to show relations.

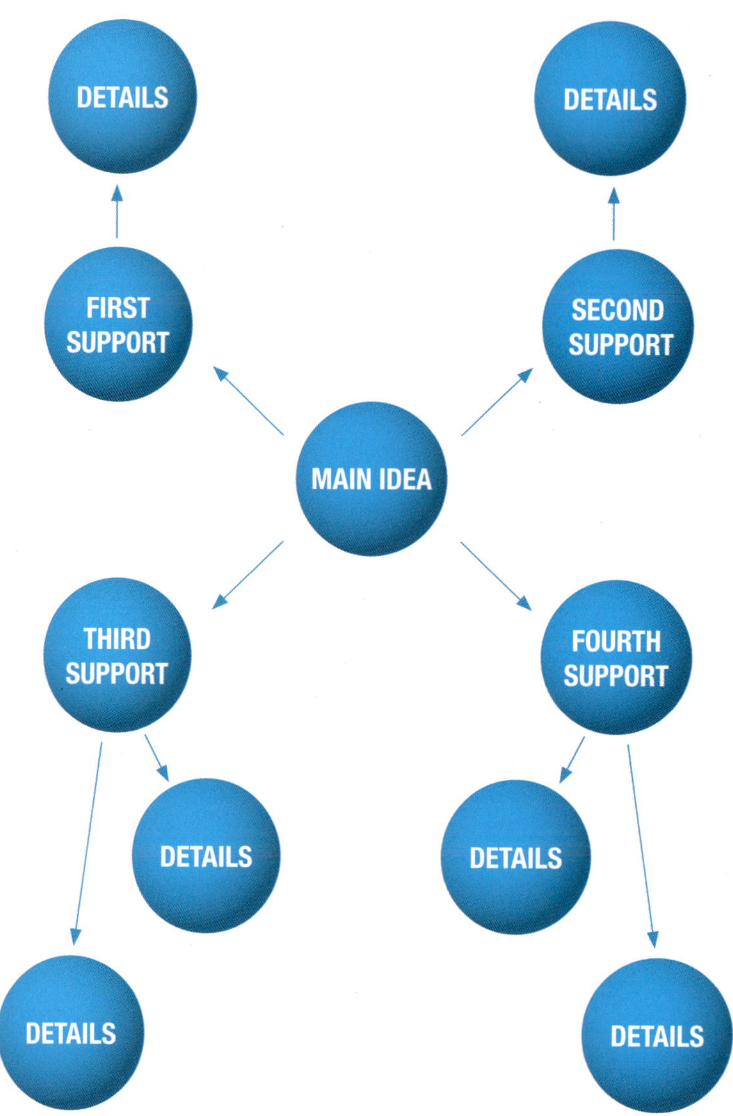

1) Exercise

Choose a narrowed topic from exercise and make a map in 10 minutes. Share with your partner and explain why you consider the circles relevant. After learning these different avenues of brainstorming–can we say there is one best way to do it. Each person is not restricted to one single way of brainstorming, some people like mapping, some like listing, while others prefer free writing. There is NO WRONG WAY. Each method has its benefits and you as the writer should use the one that you feel help you develop the most ideas.

E. Editing

Once you have developed your ideas in a map, list or through free writing, you then want to edit the list. It is during this time that you choose ideas that are most relevant or interesting for your paper topic. (remember you haven't started writing your paper yet). You can also add you ideas if you think something is important. Going back to our lists and map from the previous page, the student has crossed out ideas that she does not see as important.

1) Example editing on a list

2) Example editing on a map

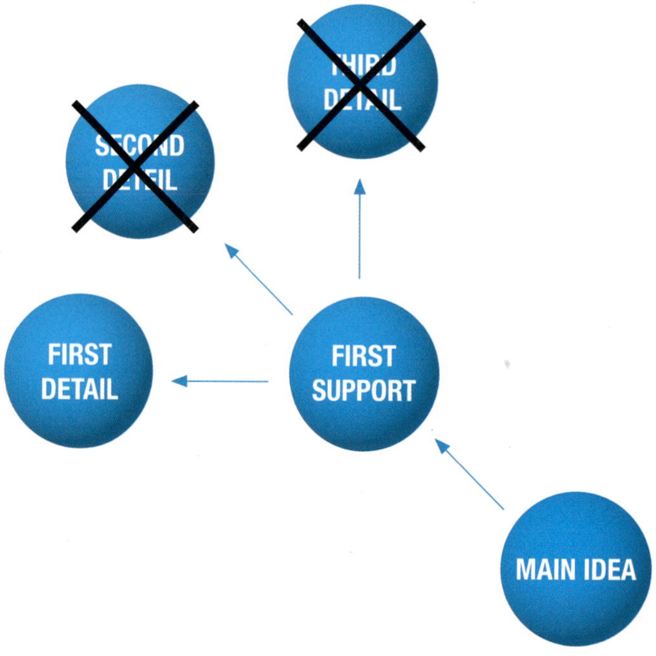

In this Map – the writer has decided that two details are not important and therefore crosses them out as not important

F. Words to know

This chapter discussed choosing and narrowing your topic. There are several important words that you should remember.

Choose	Topic	Gather	Listing
Organize	Freewriting	Prewriting	Editing

Brainstorming Mapping

4. Writing Assignments

Choose a topic that interests you and brainstorm that topic using one of the methods discussed. Talk with a partner after you have brainstormed and discuss your list or map for ideas that you may have missed or could have added.

‹‹‹ MEMO ›››

‹‹‹ MEMO ›››

‹‹‹ MEMO ›››

‹‹‹ MEMO ›››

‹‹‹ **MEMO** ›››

Let's learn English Through Sport
WRITING!

Chapter 3

Paragraph Formation

Chapter 3

Paragraph Formation

In this Chapter

In this chapter the student will understand how to define and structure a paragraph. The student will also understand how the development of a paragraph and how to identify and write a topic and conclusion sentence.

1. What is a paragraph?

paragraph is basically a collection of sentences dealing with a specific topic. These sentences when formed as a unit describe the writer's main idea. A paragraph begins with a topic sentence and then has supporting sentences. The topic sentence is the main idea and the supporting sentences are used by the writer to support or 'back up' the original idea or topic. When taken together all sentences explain the writer's main idea.

A. An example paragraph– Read the following paragraph and answer the questions.

Longtime NFL sponsor IBM, a league sponsor since 2003, has opted not to renew its league sponsorship rights, joining Motorola (SportsBusiness Journal, March 19) as another veteran sponsor deciding not to return to the NFL. While "Big Blue" is more familiar as a nickname for the New Jersey-based Super Bowl champs, the tech industry version has been a model business-to-business sponsor during its tenure as an NFL corporate sponsor, using league infrastructure projects like the digitization of NFL Films and other IT projects to demonstrate its capabilities.

1) What is the topic of the paragraph?

2) What is the main idea?

3) What are the supporting details?

B. Here is another example – read and answer the questions

No matter which aspect of society you examine, home, work, or sport, one continuing and troublesome area is the differing standards that reflect gender. Historically, women have been denied access to many areas which have been considered masculine and recognized in relation to their husbands or husbands work (Miley and Mack, 2009). This trend, according to Barletta (2003) and Silverstein et. al. (2003) is changing though with women working in greater numbers and earning higher wages than previous eras (Silverstein et. al., 2003). In education and professional jobs women are thriving, are entering the workforce in higher numbers than ever before and are earning greater salaries (Miley & Mack, 2009). These changes have encouraged more female participation in decision making processes in the workplace and outside the workplace.

1) What is the topic of this paragraph?

2) What is the main idea of the paragraph?

3) What are the supporting details?

2. Organization of a paragraph

A. What is involved in a paragraph?

1) Paragraph has three main parts

- Topic sentence – This is the writers' main idea and is usually the first sentence in any paragraph.

- Supporting sentences – This is the explanation of the topic sentence. These sentences are more detailed than the topic sentence.

- Concluding sentences – This is usually the final sentence of the paragraph and is used by the writer to repeat the main idea or as a transition to the next paragraph.

2) Here is an example of a paragraph format

The Topic Sentence →	Liverpool football club are the most successful soccer club in England. The club has won five European cups,
Supporting Details →	numerous leagues championships, over ten league cups,

and is widely recognized as producing some of the greatest young players in the game today. Liverpool football club with these successes have shown that they are without doubt the greatest soccer club in England.

Concluding sentence →

B. Read the following example paragraph and identify the topic sentence, supporting sentences, and concluding sentence.

One can see from the historical underrepresentation and trivialization of women in sport that women are still attempting to break the shackles of domesticity. This discrimination has been well documented by academics such as Eastman & Billings, 2000; Messner 1988, 1992, 1988; Sabo 1989; and Vincent, Johnson, Imwold, & Massey, 2003. Thus one area which has received little attention from academia is the role of females involved in sport consumerism. Sport consumerism is often viewed as being a male dominated activity, though according to Wann, Melnick, Russell, and Pease (2001) the number of female sport consumers is increasing. How and why females are becoming sport consumers is important because with the increased participation of women athletes at all levels of sport, there is a need to understand the influence in sport spectatorship and participation.

1) Topic Sentence:

2) Support Sentence:

3) Concluding Semtence:

C. The following are examples of paragraphs – read the paragraphs and check which one is a good paragraph. Talk with classmates to see why you think they are good paragraphs or bad paragraphs.

1) Show three examples of good and bad paragraphs

- Good or Bad

Being a great soccer player requires playing sport all the time. I played soccer for 10 years and I really like soccer. I grew up playing basketball and baseball as well as soccer but soccer is my number 1 love. Soccer is the best sport in the world with over 1 billion people play soccer on all the continents. It is my opinion that soccer will be the most popular sport in the world by 2040

- Good or Bad

Sport competitions can be traced back to the times of the Ancient Greeks. Since that time, especially in recent years, sport has become a major component of national economies and pastimes. Sports are a major part of millions of individuals' lives around the world. With this huge surge in popularity, there has been an increase in the number of new sports, new sport leagues, and new sport teams in recent years. Consequently, the competition between sports, sport teams, and sport leagues has increased dramatically. Marketers are faced with this increase in competition and are seeking ways to attract the most consumers to their product.

- Good or Bad

Sport researchers have shifted their focus from the study of demand-based variables to the study of intrapersonal motives affecting sport consumer behavior. Researching these intrapersonal motives demands the study of various sports and distinct groups of fans and spectators. Because this is such a new area of research, more studies are required for better generalizations to occur. There are too many sports not yet analyzed and in particular, there many non-revenue sports that have not been studied at all. However, marketers can begin to use the findings of the reviewed literature to help in their marketing efforts. As they begin to implement the suggested changes, no doubt new ideas will be uncovered and new research agendas can be created.

3. The Topic Sentence

The topic sentence as previously mentioned is the first sentence in a paragraph and allows the reader to understand or interpret what the writer's main idea is.

A. Circle the topic of the sentence -

1) Korea is the best soccer team in Asia.

2) Summer is the time for the Olympic Games

3) Baseball is my least favorite sport because it is boring

4) The best place to play soccer is in Suwon

B. In the following paragraphs find the topic sentence.

1) Paragraph 1

It's the first day of the MLB season and at the stadium complex in South Philadelphia, fans are lining up 2 1/2 hours before game time to watch their beloved Phillies. That may not sound that unusual, except that the Phillies opened the season 300 miles west, in Pittsburgh.However loud the crowd was that day at PNC Park, it's hard to believe it could rival the cacophony inside the newly opened Xfinity Live!, a development from partners Comcast-Spectacor and Cordish Cos. that is a sports bar on acid, combining a 24-foot-wide Sony high-definition screen in its center with a variety of indoor and outdoor dining venues across a 60,000-square-foot site in the shadow of Philadelphia's sports venues.

2) Paragraph 2

Sales of Minor League Baseball licensed merchandise climbed to near-record levels in 2011, according to data obtained by SportsBusiness Journal and scheduled to be released by MiLB today.The 160 U.S.- and Canada-based clubs affiliated with MLB teams generated $52.2 million through the sale of apparel, headwear and novelties last year, up 2 percent from 2010 and trailing only pre-recession 2008 as the highest annual total ever.

3) Paragraph 3

The 2016 Olympics sponsorship is a departure for Nike. The company historically sponsors Olympic teams, not organizing committees. It last sponsored an organizing committee in 2000 when it replaced Reebok as the official sportswear partner less than a year before the Sydney opening ceremony. Reebok had withdrawn from its sponsorship after alleging that Sydney organizers breached their contract. Within days, Nike reached an agreement with the International Olympic Committee and Sydney organizers to replace Reebok.

C. Write a topic sentence for the following topics

1) A sport team

2) An athlete

3) A sport

4) A sport event

4. Concluding sentence

The way to end a paragraph
The concluding sentence is the final sentence of a paragraph and it reviews the main authors main idea in a different way than the topic sentence. It summarizes the paragraph to highlight the main points and use different words to restate the main idea. The concluding sentence should not insert any new ideas in the paragraph.

A. From the following examples find the concluding sentence

1) Example 1

The partnership was announced a year ago and hailed in an ESPN announcement as a "new step in media transparency." Poynter staff would review ESPN's content and practices and comment as appropriate, while also addressing fan concerns and writing monthly essays. The relationship continues the ombudsman role previously held by former TV producer Don Ohlmeyer. Before him, Le Anne Schreiber, a former New York Times sports editor and author, and George Solomon, former sports editor of The Washington Post, separately held that role. With Poynter, ESPN would gain the institute's expertise in teaching and encouraging ethical behavior.

2) Example 2

In this nondisclosure, I think Poynter errs. Given its status within the journalism profession as an ethical stalwart, its transparency in this relationship should be above the letter of the law. I don't believe that Poynter is being bought off by ESPN, but I do believe that Poynter could head off any ethical misgivings while showing that it is truly the worldwide leader when it comes to journalism ethics. It takes some organizational courage to show the specific financial benefits of such relationships. That courage is buoyed by confidence that what it is doing in its work with ESPN is right.

5. Paragraph Development

What does it mean- Once the writer has decided on a topic the writer should then develop the main idea. To do this, the writer adds more information to highlight and explain the main idea. This can be done through adding details, explanations, or giving examples.

A. Details– are specific points that reinforce or support a general statement.

1) Example

The use of texting is a convenient and anonymous form of communication to quickly inform sports facility operators of an issue requiring their attention, whether it's a beverage spill, broken seat or a foul-mouthed fan.The benefit of texting for teams and crowd management firms is that fans can alert facility operators to an issue in the stands without leaving their seats to find an usher, guest services or a security worker. In Miami, for example, fans text the word "heat," the issue and seating location to a specific number. The text is sent to the arena's command center and an administrator's pager. That person is assigned to confirm the message and respond to the issue, said Kim Stone, the arena's executive vice president and general manager.Every NFL stadium now has a text message system in place, and several MLB parks have tapped into the programs provided by vendors such as GuestAssist and In Stadium Solutions. Vendors are developing newer technology that can further integrate texting into a building's incident management software system.

2) What is the topic sentence?

3) What details did the writer use?

4) What other details could you use – compare with a partner

B. Explanation– shows how something works or what something means.

1) Examples

With creative is it one message for all countries? Many messages for each country? What is the approach?

The ambition [at Coca-Cola] was one idea, one message. The way we tried to recruit teenagers was knowing, "Yes, they like the athletes." But we looked at what they are most passionate about: music.What we did was take the combination of music, London, the social side of the Games and created a story around it. We got the producer Mark Ronson, who has worked with Adele and the late Amy Winehouse, and we signed up five athletes from around the world — the U.K., the U.S., Singapore, Russia and Mexico. And then Mark Ronson brought in a young talent named Katy B and put together a song around the sound of sport. The story about Mark Ronson's journey called "Move to the Beat" is the common [creative] idea across all countries for Coca-Cola.

2) What is writer trying to explain?

3) Does the writer do a good job of explaining?

C. Examples– is a specific place, person, or event that supports the main idea or topic sentence.

1) Examples

What is the ambush temperature right now? It seemed to be there were more ambush activities around Vancouver than Beijing. What's the read going into London?

Frankly, ambush is sort of a necessary evil. If you have a strong property, a strong brand, people want to associate with that. As I look at activity for London, we're seeing on a global scale the number of submissions that have come through and will come through is almost a 1,000 percent increase from Beijing. We've taken the stance that it's much better to be proactive about ambush than reactive. A couple of steps we've taken: In December we had a congressional hearing on the Hill and we did a briefing for Congress on what exactly ambush is in the United States and how it hurts the athletes when someone tramples on our rights. We have made a huge effort to do outreach to people to make sure not only are they not ambushing intentionally but also that they know what the rules are. The rules of the Olympic movement are a little more complicated, so explaining it to people is important. Last fall, we did a sports agent workshop with the agents representing the top 150 athletes in the United States. We explained the rules and since then we've just had a lot more proactive outreach from agents saying, "

1) What example did the writer use?

2) Why did the writer use that example - explain

6. Words to know

Details explanation paragraph Development

topic sentence Support explanation example

structure.

7. Article Questions

The purpose of this study is to determine how fans come to support non-local teams. Most of our research in sport management deals with how fans support their favorite teams but does not differentiate between reasons why fans choose local versus non-local teams. Consequently, this particular piece has much to offer to our knowledge of fandom and the process by which people are attracted to certain teams.

The study was unique in that the authors used qualitative methods to obtain their data. However, in using these methods, key elements of qualitative studies were missing. If the following elements were included in the manuscript, the study would have been much more effective.

First, the authors neglected to tell the readers what qualitative perspective guided their research. There are common themes in qualitative research including grounded theory, phenomenological perspectives, and ethnography. Unfortunately the authors did not provide any discussion concerning which qualitative perspective was most appropriate for the research being conducted. One can assume the phenomenological perspective was being used which is to gain a deeper understanding of people's everyday experiences (Patton, 2002). Similarly, one could also assume grounded theory may have been used which seeks to generate theory. Although Funk and James (2001) PCM provided a good explanation of how fans become loyal to teams, it does not provide an explanation for all fans' loyalty process. The researchers for this particular study were able to identify common themes among fans of non-local teams which were never mentioned by Funk and James. Generation of these new ideas and theories would fit well into a grounded theory perspective in qualitative research.

Secondly, the researchers are faced with the issue of triangulation. Triangulation is essentially a means to strengthen a study. The researchers made weak attempts at triangulation. For example, one researcher interviewed one set of interviewees alone and then the second researcher joined for the last interview. It would have been more effective and added strength and validity to the study if both interviewers would have been present for all interview sessions. It seemed allowing a second interviewer to be present only for the final interview defeated the purpose of triangulation.

Two final problems of this study are the way fans were identified and the coding of the data. On page seven of the manuscript, the authors discuss how the fans chosen for the study must have considered the Whalers as their favorite team at one point and show "direct behavioral and attitudinal loyalty to the team." We know from the literature there are a variety of team identification scales that could have been used to validate this idea. For example, the Sport Spectator Identification Scale (Wann&Branscombe, 1993) could have been used to confirm that the teams were indeed the fans' favorite. Basically, more description is needed here as to how these fans were identified.

Lastly, there is no discussion of how the data was coded for this study. In qualitative research there are specific methods of data coding. While it is sometimes left to personal preference as to which method of data coding can be used, the study does not provide any discussion as to how or why this data was actually coded. It would be helpful to the readers if they knew just a little more about the processes the researchers used.

A. QUESTIONS

1) What is the author trying to convey to the reader?

2) Is the paragraph explained properly?

3) Does the author use supporting details within the paragraph?

4) Does the author have a strong topic sentence?

8. Writing assignment

A. Design and write a paragraph on the following topics

1) Summer Olympics

2) FIFA World Cup

3) Golf

B. From the paragraphs in section E– identify the topic sentence, support sentences, and conclusion sentence.

1) Detail Paragraph

2) Explanation Paragraph

3) Example Paragraph

‹‹‹ MEMO ›››

‹‹‹ **MEMO** ›››

‹‹‹ MEMO ›››

‹‹‹ MEMO ›››

Different types of Paragraphs

Chapter 4

Different types of Paragraphs

In this Chapter

In this unit the reader will understand the different types of paragraphs, how to organize and write, and the reasons for using different types of paragraphs

1. Descriptive paragraph

Descriptive paragraphs can tell us how things feel, look, taste, sound, and smell. Descriptive words paint a picture a readers mind and when writing a descriptive paragraph, a person should use detailed observations. The more detail used the better the potential story. The reader should be able to see the picture that you had thought about.

A. Description paragraph can answer

1) Where

- Location of people or things

2) How

- Size, feelings, temperature.

3) What

- Visuals, needs, emotions

B. From the following pictures – list words that can describe them

1) Tackle in sport

2) Winning a gold medal

C. Questions – Describe your favorite athlete

D. Questions – With a partner describe your favorite stadium

2. Opinion

In this paragraph type the writer will use facts which are pieces of information that are true to support an opinion. A fact is a soccer game officially lasts 90 minutes, while an opinion is an idea about a topic such as baseball is boring. A writer will use facts to support their opinions.

A. Fact versus Opinion - Circle the correct answer

1) LiverpoolF.C. wear red — Fact or Opinion

2) Samsung is better than LG — Fact or Opinion

3) Baseball uses umpires — Fact or Opinion

4) Soccer is boring — Fact or Opinion

5) Tennis is more fun than pool — Fact or Opinion

6) Olympics is about money — Fact or Opinion

B. Example

What was the key in selecting the athletes who are representing your brands?

I'm sure it differs by company here, but from Samsung's perspective one thing we wanted to do was diversify and have current hopefuls and former athletes and Paralympians as well. Beyond that, you have to think about fit with your brand. In this age of social, you have to be looking at things like Klout scores and how much you can project the reach and utility of who you're associating yourself with.We've selected 13 athletes — 11 current and two past Olympians. We're very careful in choosing athletes that are competitive, that have a chance of getting to the Games — that's important — that represent our brand the right way, that they were consistent with the values we thought were important, the values we're trying to inculcate in the brand.

1) What is the main idea of the paragraph?

2) What is the purpose of the paragraph?

3) What are the supporting sentences?

3. Compare and Contrast

A comparison paragraph compares two subjects, people, things, places and discusses the similarities or how much they are alike. Such as both men and women professional speed skaters need to practice a lot. A contrasting paragraph means to discuss the differences between two people, subjects, things, or places. Such as Steven Gerrard is a better midlfielder than Paul Scholes because of his skill.

A. Example Paragraph

The Boston Red Sox own an MLB-record 737-games-and-counting sellout streak at Fenway Park, and the Philadelphia Phillies are second-best in the sport with an active streak of 228 straight games at Citizens Bank Park, both through May 29. Both, however, sat in last place in their respective divisions at press time.Amid their respective on-field woes and player injuries, empty seats have become much more frequent sights at both ballparks, a startling reversal from years of regularly packed houses.

Both the Red Sox and Phillies acknowledged no-show rates increased in the season's early going, especially for weekday and weeknight games and those played in uncertain weather. The Red Sox's no-show rate now stands at 13.6 percent, roughly equal to a similar point last year, and the club's season-ticket renewals and single-game advance ticket sales each are slightly trailing last year's pace.As the empty seats have multiplied, local media in Boston most notably have called the integrity of the Fenway Park streak into question, in part pointing to the inclusion of complimentary tickets in the totals. Similar questions have been raised to a lesser degree in Philadelphia, and the Phillies last week employed a buy-one-get-one-free ticket offer for certain seats to Wednesday's game against the Los Angeles Dodgers. "The inquiries are understandable and natural. The visual isn't always good," said Sam Kennedy, Red Sox chief operating officer. "So we have certainly seen an influx of questions so far this year on how we're doing selling tickets. And fortunately, the answer on a game-by-game basis on the primary market is that we're still doing well, and I'm very optimistic about the summer."

B. Organization of comparing and contrasting

1) There are two methods –one is the point by point paragraph method and the other is the blocked paragraph method.

2) Point by point compares and contrasts the topic point by point. First, contrast both topics (A and B) then discuss the first point about A and B, then talk about the second point about A and B., then the next point of A and B and so on.

3) Point by Point

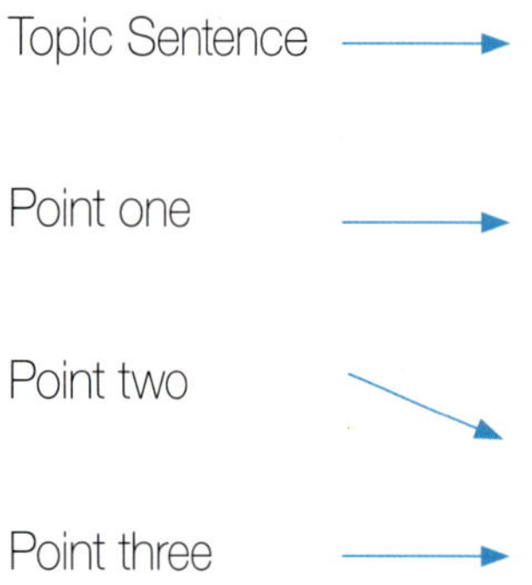

Steven Gerrard and Paul Scholes play for different soccer teams but both play with similar styles. Both players are fantastic passers of the ball and can pick a player out from anywhere on the field. Also, both players have an intense sense of pride playing for their teams and country. Another similarity is that both players are very supportive of their teammates and always try to be positive towards

Concluding sentence →	them even after mistakes. Gerrard and Scholes both continue to play at the top level and do so because they both have the desire to see their team succeed and be the greatest in the league.

4) Block paragraph discusses one topic and then the next section of the paragraph discusses the other subject that is to be compared or contrasted with the first. The conclusion then puts what your comparing or contrasting together.

Topic Sentence →	Watching a sporting event is much different than watching it on television.
Point one →	When you watch it in person, you can feel the atmosphere of fans around you and feel the passion that people have for the game. You get to hear songs and sing with your fellow supporters.
Point two →	Watching on television may be easier but you do not get the same experience. You do not get to see the games excitement in real time, you do not get to experience the emotional rollercoaster that fellow fans experience.
Concluding sentence →	While both games are the same, the experiences are much different.

5) What are the similarities and differences between the following sports

- Soccer Basketball
- Golf Tennis
- Skating Curling
- Badminton Squash

4. Problem and solution

This paragraph explains what the issue is and then provides a solution to that issue. So the writer will state and define the problem, then suggest possible solutions and finally evaluate the solutions for recommendations

A. Read the following paragraph and answer the questions

Congratulations! You're the director of marketing for a major soft drink and you just signed an agreement to sponsor a professional sports team. Your agreement states that your brand is the team's exclusive soft drink sponsor and that no other soft drinks will be signed as team sponsors. Sounds like an airtight deal, right?Not in today's world. For example, what if the team has a beer sponsor who later acquires a competing soft drink brand? Or what if a competing soft drink wants to sponsor the team's stadium (but not the team)? Or what if a competing soft drink wants to sponsor the brand-new online broadcasts of the team's games? Issues such as these are becoming more common in today's sports sponsorship landscape. Failure to adequately address them up front may reduce the value of your brand's sponsorship, lead to conflicts between sponsors and teams or leagues, and result in potentially costly legal battles (as evidenced by the litigation between AT&T and NASCAR over competitive sponsorship issues).In order to create a solid sponsorship agreement, parties need to recognize and address the likely issues and draft carefully for as many contingencies as possible, including defining competing brands and exclusivity.

1) What is the main idea?

2) What is the topic sentence?

3) What are the supporting ideas?

4) What solutions does the writer provide?

B. Hooligans are a major problem in many countries in Europe at soccer games

1) How would you solve the problem of hooliganism?

C. How to write a problem paragraph

1) First the topic sentence should state or name the issue you will discuss and then the supporting sentences show why the writer considers it a problem.

2) Examples:

- Sport Violence

- Steroids

- Fan violence

D. Work with a partner or group – discuss why these are considered problems

5. Linking solutions with problems

The first paragraph normally conveys the problem or explains the problem. The next paragraph should provide or explain the solution. The writer should provide support for the solution

A. Examples links

1) One answer is...

2) One solution is....

3) To solve these problems...

4) To overcome these problems

5) To limit these concerns

B. Article Example

One solution to this definitional problem is to use a definition that is indexed to a third-party categorization system that updates as new brands enter the market. For instance, a soft drink sponsor might identify a categorization system used by the beverage industry. Defining "competitor" as any brand that falls into a certain category in that system would ensure that both parties understood exactly which brands were included as competitors up front while also ensuring that new brands entering the market would be covered as competitors.

In addition to carefully defining what a competitive sponsor is, your company may want to contract against a clashing sponsor, i.e., sponsors that are not competitive in the traditional sense but that might be embarrassing or otherwise counter to the goals of the existing sponsor. For instance, a candy bar sponsor might see its sponsorship value decrease if a weight loss company became a fellow sponsor. While certain clashing sponsors could be easily named in the sponsorship agreement, others might be hard to anticipate.

Finally, sponsorship agreements need to consider issues related to multifaceted companies and corporate mergers and acquisitions. For instance, if a noncompeting sponsor acquires or is acquired by a company that is competitive with your brand, your company needs to have provisions that minimize exposure of the competitive aspect of the other sponsor. Similarly, if a noncompeting sponsor has a subsidiary that is competitive with your brand, your sponsorship agreements need to be clear that only the noncompeting parent brand may be used in connection with the sponsorship.

C. Questions

1) Circle the linking phrases

2) Underline the supporting sentences

6. Words to know

Paragraph	Description	Opinion
Compare	Contrast	Problem
Solution	Block	Point

7. Article Questions

How sports organizations can protect copyrighted content online

Highlights of sports' key moments can be uploaded and viewed repeatedly on sites like YouTube.

Copyright owners: Don't expect website providers such as YouTube to go out of their way to help you protect your copyrights any time soon, because according to recent case law, the burden is on you.

On June 23, fans of YouTube and file-sharing generally rejoiced, while copyright owners experienced a significant setback in enforcing their copyrights. On that day, the U.S. District Court for the Southern District of New York threw out a billion-dollar copyright infringement lawsuit against YouTube and its parent company, Google.

The allegations against YouTube were that, essentially, YouTube makes copyright infringement easy and attractive, and it does so in order to profit handsomely from the misuse of the copyrighted works that it knows is rampant and ongoing on its site. The plaintiffs, led by Viacom, demanded that YouTube should be forced to police its own website and take down infringing content on its own rather than place the onus on the copyright owners to notify YouTube of the infringing activity, an expensive and time-consuming proposition.

YouTube already aggressively polices its website with respect to pornography, so the plaintiffs alleged that it could easily do the same for copyright-protected works. But the federal district court determined that the plain terms of the Digital Millennium Copyright Act (DMCA) don't require site providers to go that far.

This issue is particularly important to sports organizations because of the nature of some of their most valuable copyrighted works. Sports highlights are attractive content to be uploaded and viewed on sites such as YouTube. The most valuable video content in sports might be only a few seconds of an entire match, game or bout, like the few minutes leading up to the goal that won the 2010 FIFA World Cup for Spain, or the final 10 seconds of Michael Jordan's last game with the Chicago Bulls in Game 6 of the 1998 NBA Finals. Or the final 15 seconds of the 1980 Olympic hockey semifinals, where the decidedly ragtag, underdog U.S. team beat the favored Soviet Union 4-3.

There are certain memorable moments in each game, match or bout that generate buzz and excitement for an organization. It is in these moments that history is made and fans everywhere are drawn to watch a brilliant play over and over again. Inevitably, it is these most-valuable snippets that get uploaded to YouTube. Check it out. As of printing, the examples cited earlier can be found on YouTube, in numerous iterations. You can even see how many times each has been viewed previously.

This is a serious problem for many sports organizations, as their copyrighted content is easily pirated on sites such as YouTube. Anyone can post on YouTube, and the same clip can be posted an endless number of times. The proliferation of social media has only magnified the problem, allowing users of MySpace, Facebook, blogs and other websites to imbed YouTube videos directly into their pages.

A related concern is the ease with which real-time broadcasts can be uploaded and distributed over the Internet. Pay-per-view events, for example, are most valuable in real time. When these broadcasts are streamed for free over the Internet, sports organizations lose millions of dollars. While YouTube and other similarly situated sites usually (and are required to) have a mechanism that allows copyright owners to flag infringing content and bring it to the site providers' attention, it sometimes takes days for the site provider to respond and take down the infringing material. By that time, irreparable damage has occurred.

For now, federal copyright law does not require site providers to police their own sites. As long as they provide a mechanism whereby copyright holders can request takedowns, and then they follow through with the takedowns, they will be protected under the safe harbor provisions of the DMCA with very little, if not zero, legal incentive to self-police their sites.

But the length of time involved in actually getting video content taken down can have severe consequences, particularly when applied to pirated video streaming of real-time content (such as pay-per-view broadcasts).

So what is the solution? Sports organizations may be able to strike deals with site providers allowing copyright owners to have certain web-master take-down privileges, such that a copyright owner can exercise self-help, in a sense, and not have to rely on the site providers' staff to get the job done.

More generally, copyright enforcement can take up a large amount of an organization's time and resources. The good news is that there are companies that provide copyright enforcement services. Depending upon your particular needs, these companies might be able to perform valuable protection services at lower costs than relying on internal staff.

The upshot to all of this is that YouTube and similar sites have exponentially increased the visibility of copyright owners' works to the public, and one could argue that this increased visibility is great marketing. It also appears that YouTube changed many of its policies after Google came into the picture and is now more willing to work with copyright owners to achieve workable solutions.

Like most other problems in business, resorting to the courts for copyright enforcement should be a last-ditch effort, as there are often cheaper and more efficient alternatives out there.

8. QUESTIONS

A. What is the author trying to convey to the reader?

B. What paragraphformat does the author use?

C. Does the author use supporting details within the paragraph?

D. Does the author have a strong introduction and conclusion?

9. Assignments

A. Write a compare and contrast paragraph

B. Write a problem / solution paragraph

C. Write a descriptive paragraph

‹‹‹ **MEMO** ›››

‹‹‹ MEMO ›››

<<< MEMO >>>

‹‹‹ MEMO ›››

‹‹‹ MEMO ›››

Let's learn English Through Sport
WRITING!

Chapter 5

From Paragraph to Essay

Chapter 5

From Paragraph to Essay

In this unit the reader will understand how to define an essay, format an essay and write a thesis statement.

1. What is an Essay

An essay is several paragraphs that are grouped together in a particular format that focus on a single topic or idea. The general format for an essay is a 3-5 paragraph format

2. Structure of an essay

A. Three parts

1) Introduction

- This is the first part of an essay and is usually where the writer explains the topic with general ideas. It also has a thesis statement, which is the main idea of the essay.

2) Body

- This section is where the writer will use paragraphs to explain or support the thesis statement or main idea. There are usually three paragraphs within the body and they are placed between the introduction and conclusion.

3) Conclusion

- This section is the last paragraph of the essay and it is where the writer will summarize or restate the main idea and support ideas within the essay

B. Format

1) The general format of an essay includesrules that include

- Each line should be double spaced
- Specific margins (one inch)
- Indent each new paragraph (first sentence of each new paragraph)
- Do not include pictures
- Times new roman – 12pt
- Center title at the top of your essay

2) Examples of essay formats

Like last week's article, the article for this week has much to offer to the field of Sport Management. With so many internships in our field, it is important to assess the efficacy of those internships and what affects they may have on the interns themselves. Some serious flaws in this article however limit its usefulness.

First, it appears the author does not define the key variables in the study. Affective occupational commitment, for example, was never fully defined. If any readers were unfamiliar with the concept, they would have to do research on their own. Additionally, anticipated career success was defined in terms of satisfaction but the author offers no evidence or past research indicating how the various dimensions of anticipated career success are applicable to this research agenda. It is almost as if the author just makes a statement and then goes to the next idea without substantial discussion and review.

The entire participant selection for this study was slightly confusing. It says data were gathered from upper-level undergraduate Sport Management students, but "how" was this data gathered? Were the students selected randomly? Were they in certain classes? More information is needed here. Also, it was unclear to me what "students yet to complete their internship" meant. Are these students who are actually in the internship right now but are not finished or are they waiting to begin their internship and have no experience at all? Later in the article the author refers to those students as "non-interns" and this would have been beneficial for readers near the beginning of the article.

Lastly, the author refers to his control group, but s/he offers no explanation on how job challenge and supervisor support were controlled. This is important and once again, the readers are left to infer what went on. Addressing these issues will make for a much better article.

From the above essay, you can see that the format has an introduction, a body (middle 2 paragraphs) and a conclusion – this is a good formatted essay

3. Thesis Statement

A. A thesis statement is a sentence that states the main idea of the writers' essay. This sentence is similar to a topic sentence (main idea of a paragraph) and should set the theme for your paper and is an important part of essay writing

B. What to avoid

1) Generalized statements

- Explain with example

2) Only facts

- Explain with example

3) Poor arguments or very opinionated

- Explain with example

B. Examples of thesis statement

With the NBA playoffs under way, look for a high volume of the marketing activity from league sponsors to be digitally focused.NBA data shows that more fans are engaging with the league digitally, so much of the marketing will be Web-based. Emilio Collins, the league's senior vice president of global marketing. It's the playoffs, and the NBA would like a word with you — several, actually — as part of its "Big" ad campaignpartnerships, cited a 74 percent annual increase in video downloads on NBA sites as an indication of the digital stampede.Nike is bringing back its "Epic" ad and social media campaign tied to its Facebook page. A "How Do You Keep Your Cool?" Facebook promo from Dial's Right Guard solicits consumer examples of "coolness," offering NBA Finals tickets as a top prize. American Express will tie into TNT's live streaming of playoff games, while wireless sponsor Sprint is backing an online playoff brackets game on NBA.com in which fans select top highlights with an All-Star Game trip layered in as a prize.

1) Questions

- What is the thesis statement

- What are the supporting ideas

- Write a thesis statement for your favorite sport

4. Essay Outline

A. What is an outline?

An outline is a structured organization of your essay and is usually done before you start writing to help the writer stay focused and on topic.
Shows the breakdown of the introduction

1) Thesis statement

2) Shows the organization of the body paragraphs

- Details

- Supporting sentences

3) Shows the conclusion

- Restate thesis and support

B. How to write an outline

1) Prior to writing the outline the writer should have followed the pre-writing basics. Once the author has chosen a topic, research the ideas and main points – the author then begins to organize them to form an essay.

2) The first thing a writer should do is number the paragraphs so to limit confusion later in the outline. The writer should utilize different numbers for each level of support, again this limits the confusion

3) Example one – An overall organizational plan of an essay

- Introduction

- 1st Main idea

- 2nd main idea

- 3rd main idea

- Conclusion

4) Next fill in more information for your specific paragraphs. Your body paragraphs will generally begin to have more levels as you provide more support for your main idea within the paragraph

- Introduction

- 1st main idea

- 1st supporting point

- 2nd supporting point

- 2nd main idea

- 1st supporting point

- 2nd supporting point

- 3rd main idea

- 1st supporting point

- 2nd supporting point

- Conclusion

5) Next fill in more information for your main idea and supporting points. These body paragraphs will begin to have specific points that are used to support the main ideas – Each paragraph WILL HAVE ONLY ONE MAIN IDEA and several supporting points.

- Introduction

- 1st main idea

- 1st supporting point

- First detail

- Second detail

- 2nd supporting point

- First detail

- Second detail

- 2nd main idea

- 1st supporting point

- First detail

- Second detail

- 2nd supporting point

- First detail

- Second detail

- 3rd main idea

- 1st supporting point

- First detail

- Second detail

- 2nd supporting point

- First detail

- Second detail

- Conclusion

5. Example Essay)

At first glance and after reading the abstract, one would believe the article will provide readers with a better understanding of the justification of hosting sport events and building new stadiums. Also, one would think the authors will clearly assess the evidence regarding whether sport events and stadiums have a substantial economic impact on cities. While the introduction and literature review was helpful, in the end, readers are left wondering what the main purpose of the article really was.

Initially, the authors provide a discussion on sport economic impact in different countries, the UK and the US. They correctly show how sporting events were often used in the past to revive industrial cities economically. Apparently, the goal of recent sport managers was to use sporting events as a means to lure tourists to previously run-down cities with little or no tourism. The authors then provide examples of cities in both the US and the UK where the sporting facilities and events did have a positive economic impact on cities. Barcelona for example, saw a huge increase in tourism ever since they hosted the Olympic Games. This is indeed a good example, but I believe a more in depth analysis of exactly why Barcelona's tourism industry increased so significantly would have made for a better overall article.

The idea of the article is interesting and would provide useful information to the field of Sport Management. Examining the concept of economic impact and how cities are able to use sport facilities and events to "regenerate" themselves is a valid research idea. If the authors accomplished what I believe they sought out to do – to analyze the justification for cities' investments in sport facilities and the hosting of sport events – the article would have certainly provided a good understanding of how cities can potentially reap economic benefits from sport involvement. A few key concepts were mentioned which directly apply to economic analysis. The exclusion of local residents is discussed. This concept is one of the main principles of economic analysis and is one of the few strengths of the article. Additionally, there is a discussion of how sport events and facilities will create new job opportunities for local residents. However, other important principles, such as the exclusion of "time-switchers" and "casuals," and the multiplier concept are never mentioned. I think these principles should be included in any discussion or analysis of economic impact.

Building intricate, attractive sport facilities may have an impact on the economic regeneration of a city. Perhaps hosting an international event, such as the World Cup or the Olympic Games, will increase tourism in a city for years to come. Unfortunately, measuring such effects is quite difficult. City officials and sport managers must be able to provide an unbiased analysis of exactly what is generated to the city as a direct result of a sport facility or event. Additionally, an economic analysis should take into account any intangible benefits, such as community pride, as a result of hosting an event or constructing a new facility. Gratton et al.'s article does provide good thoughts and ideas, but those ideas are unfortunately not explained sufficiently and other key ideas are completely omitted.

From the above essay answer the following questions

A. What is the author trying to convey to the reader?

B. Does the author use the correct format?

C. Does the author use supporting details for their introduction?

D. Is it and good essay – explain your answer.

6. Words to know

Supporting	Main idea	Details
Essay	Introduction	Body
Conclusion	Format	

7. Article Questions

Merchandise a powerful activation tool for teams, sponsors

The value of sports sponsorships is rooted in the strong emotional attachments fans develop with their favorite leagues, teams and athletes. It's our job as marketers to create lasting promotional ties that inspire the consumer to transfer some of that loyalty over to the sponsor.

Photo by: OAKLAND ATHLETICS

The influx of sponsorship dollars isn't expected to slow in the foreseeable future. In its December 2011 forecast "Changing the Game," PricewaterhouseCoopers projected global revenue from sponsorships will account for the largest share of the sports market's $146 billion estimated revenue in 2014. Sponsorship is the fastest-growing sector in the sports market, with an expected global compound annual growth rate of 5.3 percent from 2011 to 2015.

Nowhere is this growth more evident than with branded merchandise, an advertising medium that's steadily gaining traction among sports entities and the world's most iconic corporate brands. While network television, radio, magazine and newspaper ad spending all decreased last year, according to Kantar Media, the Advertising Specialty Institute reported sales growth of 6.2 percent in 2011 to more than $18.5 billion. That's on the heels of a 9 percent increase.

Branded merchandise giveaways are three-dimensional ads that go home with the fan.
Photo by: MLB NETWORK

Merchandise provides both teams and sponsors a powerful activation vehicle because it brings their brands to life. It works in concert with a sponsor's stadium signage, TV spots and print campaigns. It lets people see, touch, feel, own and interact with a brand in a way no other medium permits. Gifted campaign strategists realize that with merchandise, the brand messaging doesn't turn off — and it can drive fan behavior and activation.

Of course, there are critics of merchandise because it's so pervasive in our society. The easy label is tchotchke, trinket or trash. But smart teams and sponsors understand product placement doesn't get more personal than branded merchandise. It's three-dimensional advertising that goes home with the fan.

You'll see it play out all summer long in MLB ballparks. Looking at the promotional schedules of 29 of the 30 MLB teams (the Boston Red Sox don't release one), there are more than 700 merchandise giveaways slated for the 2012 season. The Pittsburgh Pirates lead the way, with merchandise activations attached to 43 of their 81 home games, while another 13 teams have 25 or more giveaways on tap. Only three clubs (Toronto Blue Jays, Atlanta Braves and San Diego Padres) show fewer than 12 giveaways on their published schedules.

It's widely accepted around the league that teams should expect a jolt in ticket sales from a well-executed giveaway of high-perceived value. More importantly, these fans are taking home a souvenir with a sponsor's logo they'll either wear, display or put to use in their daily lives — driving additional brand impressions and loyalty.

We heard firsthand accounts of the impact a merchandise activation can have on attendance and the overall game-day experience from team officials during our 17th annual Baseball Think Tank this past offseason. BDA brings together the top marketing minds from MLB each November to share best practices; discuss product trends for in-stadium giveaways and ticket renewal premiums; review the latest importing, safety testing and compliance standards; and strategize ways to continually improve fan experiences.

Gregg Greene, the Seattle Mariners' director of marketing, put it best.

"A great giveaway can create lines at the ballpark as well as added value and affinity with the Mariners brand," he said. "It doesn't matter if it's a Little Leaguer or a CEO. The right collectible or gear creates that moment at the ballpark when the fan thinks, 'Wow, this is really cool. I want to put this in my office. I want to wear this.' That's something that no other form of advertising can offer. Sports is about creating moments, and I think giveaways help fans celebrate those moments well beyond the event they attended."

The San Francisco Giants are a team that sees how a merchandise activation can help bridge the gap between a casual fan and an avid fan. With every person who comes out to AT&T Park as part of a community group or due to a specific promotion, there's an opportunity to make a lasting impression. Handing out Gigantes T-shirts during Hispanic Heritage Month or neon orange snap watches to the younger set is a simple first step in building a connection between the fan, team and sponsor — not to mention the brand exposure generated every time those fans wear their new favorite shirt or wristwatch.

MLB Network also recognizes there's considerable ROI to gain from merchandise. The 3-year-old network is giving away 685,000 drawstring sports bags featuring its logo in 27 ballparks this season. Mary Beck, senior vice president of marketing and promotion for MLB Network, lobbied for a leaguewide merchandise activation from the early days of the network.

"Merchandise is an important component of MLB Network's marketing efforts as it makes our brand tangible and promotes awareness to baseball fans — the largest push this year being an MLB Network Giveaway Day," she said. "We view this as a great way to increase recognition of the network among avid baseball fans."

For good reason.

Today's consumer pays close attention to who's behind a giveaway. In a survey commissioned by ASI, 83 percent of U.S. respondents indicated they could identify the advertiser on a promotional item they owned, and 41 percent said their opinion of the advertiser was more favorable after receiving a promotional product.

Add in the fact that avid sports fans are supportive to brands associated with their favorite leagues and teams. Advertisers capitalize on this loyalty by giving fans merchandise that lets them show off their team pride, and sponsors are part of this equation in a very visible, tangible way. When branding is done well, it is seamless and well-received by fans of all demographics.

Whether it's custom earrings for every mom on Mother's Day, kid-friendly collectibles, or 40,000 rally towels waving like crazy down to the final out of the playoffs, merchandise activations help expand the fan experience. The right piece of merchandise turns spectators into lifelong brand ambassadors. It extends brand messaging beyond any single game, event or venue — directly into people's hearts and homes.

8. QUESTIONS

A. What is the author trying to convey to the reader?

B. Does the author use the correct format for the paragraphs?

C. Does the author use supporting details within the paragraph?

D. Does the author have a strong introduction and conclusion?

9. Writing assignment

A. Write an outline on one of the following topics or choose your own

1) Steroids in sport

2) Gambling in sport

3) Violence in sport

4) Gender and sport

5)

‹‹‹ MEMO ›››

<<< MEMO >>>

‹‹‹ **MEMO** ›››

‹‹‹ **MEMO** ›››

Let's learn English Through Sport
WRITING!

Chapter 6

The Importance of Introductions and Conclusions

Chapter 6

The Importance of Introductions and Conclusions

In this unit the reader will understand the purpose of an introduction and the purpose of a conclusion. The Introduction and conclusion are important to the overall essay because they allow the reader to understand what the essay is about (the introduction) and the summary of the paper or final comment of the papers importance (the conclusion).

1. Introductions

A. What is an introduction

1) IS the first paragraph of an essay and is usually a paragraph to catch interest of the reader. It is also a paragraph that states the general idea of the essay and states the main thesis statement

2) Example: You generate your thesis from the general idea of your paper

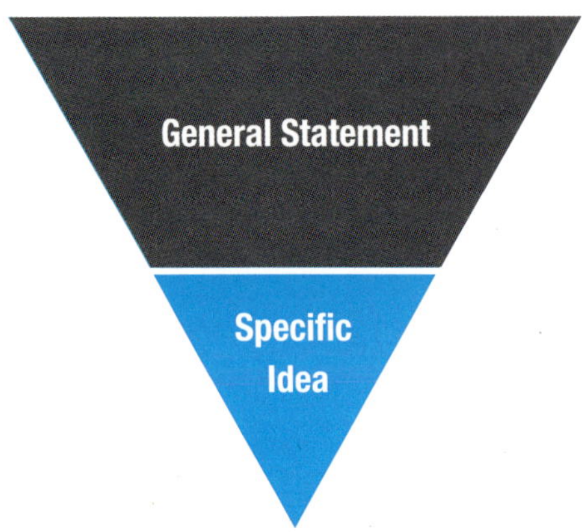

3) General Statement'

- Soccer is popular

- Samsung is better than LG in electronics

- China has the greatest Olympic Athletes

4) Now right a thesis statement for each of these:

B. How to write a strong introduction

1) A strong introduction should do the following

- Be clear

- Provide information on the topic

- State the main idea

- Only talk about the main topic

2) Examples

- Which of the following is a good or bad introduction?

- Example one

Corporate social responsibility (CSR) is a common term in today's business world. A search of "corporate social responsibility" on Google Scholar reveals more than 409,000 scholarly articles on the construct. Furthermore, an identical search on Google reveals more than 25 million hits. The copious amount of literature and research on this subject is apparent from these brief searches. It seems all companies around the globe are familiar with CSR and in recent years, most have begun to engage in some type of CSR practice. Sport organizations are no different. Extejt (2004) reports 66% of professional sport teams in four major leagues in the United States (Major League Baseball, National Football League, National Hockey League, National Basketball League) host a type of charitable foundation.

Circle the thesis statement

- Example two

Just after Thanksgiving in 1987, I received a call from John Houston. It was unexpected and one of those many calls that I had learned to adjust to. John explained that his daughter, Whitney Houston, had just fired her manager. As her new manager, he had learned that she was booked to perform the national anthem at Super Bowl XXII, which was a little more than two months away. No one else was aware of this, he said, and they had a previous commitment to tour Australia. So began a 16-year relationship with John Houston.

Circle the thesis statement

- Example three

Just after Thanksgiving in 1987, I received a call from John Houston. It was unexpected and one of those many calls that I had learned to adjust to. John explained that his daughter, Whitney Houston, had just fired her manager. As her new manager, he had learned that she was booked to perform the national anthem at Super Bowl XXII, which was a little more than two months away. No one else was aware of this, he said, and they had a previous commitment to tour Australia. So began a 16-year relationship with John Houston.

Circle the thesis statement

- Example four

Public subsidies for professional sport facilities are a major issue for sport teams, potential host cities, team owners, and tax payers. As evident from our past readings, the different eras in sport facility financing (Gestation Era, Public Subsidy Era, Transitional Era, and the Fully-Loaded Era) has changed dramatically since the early 1960's. Over the past 40 years, there has been a gradual increase in the public's subsidization of sport facilities. Friedman and Mason provide a stakeholder analysis model to help determine which groups have the most influence on policies and procedures regarding public stadium financing.

Circle the thesis statement

- Example five

The value of sports sponsorships is rooted in the strong emotional attachments fans develop with their favorite leagues, teams and athletes. It's our job as marketers to create lasting promotional ties that inspire the consumer to transfer some of that loyalty over to the sponsor.The influx of sponsorship dollars isn't expected to slow in the foreseeable future. In its December 2011 forecast "Changing the Game," PricewaterhouseCoopers projected global revenue from sponsorships will account for the largest share of the sports market's $146 billion estimated revenue in 2014.

Sponsorship is the fastest-growing sector in the sports market, with an expected global compound annual growth rate of 5.3 percent from 2011 to 2015.

Circle the thesis statement

2. Conclusion

A conclusion is important to give the reader a review of the main points of the essay and/or to provide guidance for any actions that should be taken within the essay. A strong conclusion can give the reader a greater overview of the main idea of the paper when the writer does not introduce new topics or ideas – so never introduce new ideas in the conclusion

A. A strong conclusion should do the following

1) Summarize main points–

- Restate thesis
- Look at the essay from page
- Does the conclusion summarize the main points

- Does the conclusion restate the main idea

- Are any new ideas introduced?

B. The following are examples of conclusions – which ones are good or bad?

1) Example 1

- Circle good or bad

One final point presented is how to decrease the emphasis of short-term gains by investors and corporation stakeholders associated with the stock market. She argues value should be placed on non-financial returns to begin making this change. I am not sure if this is a feasible idea. In our society it is expected for organizations to be socially responsible but at the same time, the real reason corporations exist is to make money.

2) Example 2

- Circle good or bad

Whether it's custom earrings for every mom on Mother's Day, kid-friendly collectibles, or 40,000 rally towels waving like crazy down to the final out of the playoffs, merchandise activations help expand the fan experience. The right piece of merchandise turns spectators into lifelong brand ambassadors. It extends brand messaging beyond any single game, event or venue — directly into people's hearts and homes.

3) Example 3

- Circle good or bad

Moreover, creating a sports news media franchise optimized for a four-screen, socially connected world presents an extraordinary opportunity to redefine the industry. It might be intriguing enough to entice cash-rich, nontraditional media players like Apple, Facebook or Google to mount a challenge.It will take time, but perhaps the mountain isn't as high as we think. Remember, "American Idol" seemed unstoppable in 2010. Now, it's chasing "The Voice."

4) Example 4

- Circle good or bad

Sports are one of the last examples of our town squares. Stadiums and ballparks serve as rallying points for increasingly diverse and financially fragmented communities. These massive meeting places are the front porch of days gone by.

But as the skyboxification of our favorite stadiums and arenas falls into the hands of the sports-revenue metricists, we are losing the glue of unity that binds us together as fans. Sport stadiums are increasingly getter bigger and becoming more popular with businesses for meetings. You can even bring new employees there to see if you enjoy their company. Stadiums are the future

3. Words to know

Introductions	Conclusions	General
Specific	Summary	Restate

4. Article Reading

Nike scores in Brazil with '16 Olympic deal

By Tripp Mickle&Terry Lefton, Staff Writers

Published April 2, 2012, Page 1

Font Size Resize Small Resize Normal Resize Large | Print | Share |

Nike has signed a sponsorship agreement with Rio 2016 and the Brazilian national team, scoring a major corporate victory in the race for market share in fast-growing Brazil.

The deal gives Nike its first official Olympic organizing committee sponsorship since the 2000 Sydney Games. It represents a tremendous opportunity to strengthen Nike's brand positioning in Brazil and generate strong licensed merchandise sales on the back of Brazil's emerging middle class.

Under terms of the four-year deal, Nike will receive marketing and licensing rights to the Rio Games. It also will outfit all Brazilian national teams (except volleyball, which is sponsored by Olympikus) for the 2012 London and 2016 Rio Games. Unlike most Olympic apparel partners, Nike won't outfit volunteers working at the Rio Games, and it is still being determined if it will provide opening and closing ceremony apparel for the Brazilian team, sources familiar with the deal said.

Financial terms weren't available, but sources valued the deal in the $25 million to $40 million range. The total is significantly less than Rio organizers could have gotten for the deal.

Rio organizers opted to take Nike's tier-three sponsorship offer over a tier-one sponsorship proposal from the Brazilian sportswear brand Olympikus, which is owned by VulcabrasAzaleia. In doing so, it is expected to become the first organizing committee to split team and volunteer outfitting into separate categories. They are expected to begin searching for a volunteer outfitting sponsor later this year, but it's unclear where the organizing committee will turn to find an outfitter for that workforce.

Adidas paid $127 million for a tier-one sponsorship agreement for the 2012 London Games. But Brazil needed an outfitter for its national teams for the upcoming London Games, and sources said it chose Nike because of its reputation for product innovation.

Adidas, the official sportswear partner of the Athens, Beijing and London Games, did not compete for the Rio 2016 sponsorship. As an official FIFA partner, the company will have a dominant position in Brazil during the 2014 World Cup.

Rio 2016 already has signed five tier-one sponsorships and surpassed its goal of raising $570 million in sponsorship revenue. The organizer's last tier-one deal with Nissan reportedly was worth $250 million. Its other tier-one partners are Bradesco, BradescoSeguros, Claro and Embratel. It has a tier-two sponsorship with Ernst & Young.

The 2016 Olympics sponsorship is a departure for Nike. The company historically sponsors Olympic teams, not organizing committees. It last sponsored an organizing committee in 2000 when it replaced Reebok as the official sportswear partner less than a year before the Sydney opening ceremony. Reebok had withdrawn from its sponsorship after alleging that Sydney organizers breached their contract. Within days, Nike reached an agreement with the International Olympic Committee and Sydney organizers to replace Reebok.

Though the deal for the 2000 Olympics was cut hastily, Nike benefited from strong licensed product sales during the Games. Sources close to the deal with Rio 2016 said the company expects licensed product sales during those Olympics to be huge because of the growth of the Brazilian middle class and worldwide interest in Rio. Organizers of the 2016 Olympics projected more than $50 million in licensed merchandise sales in their IOC bid in 2008.

The deal included two other appealing components for Nike. First, it will be the dominant brand worn by Brazilian athletes in every sport from sailing and tae kwon do to track and field and soccer, which it already outfitted. Second, it doesn't require the company, as is customary, to outfit the 50,000-plus volunteers who work an Olympics. That gives Nike the assurance, which the company prefers, that its brand will only be featured on athletes.

A. QUESTIONS

1) What is the author trying to convey to the reader?

2) Does the author use good format for the paragraphs

3) Does the author use supporting details within the paragraph

4) Does the author have a strong introduction and conclusion?

5. Writing assignment

A. Write an introduction and conclusion for the following topics

1) Drugs should be banned from sports

2) Women should be allowed to play men's sports

3) Korea should host the 2026 FIFA World cup

4) Korean athletes should be exempt from Military service

B. Compare with a partner and discuss why you think it is a good or bad effort

‹‹‹ MEMO ›››

‹‹‹ **MEMO** ›››

‹‹‹ MEMO ›››

‹‹‹ MEMO ›››

Let's learn English Through Sport
WRITING!

Chapter 7
Different types of Essays

Chapter 7

Different types of Essays

In this unit the reader will understand the different types of essays and when to use them. There are several types of essays but in this chapter we will focus on what we consider the most popular and those are

- Descriptive
- Compare/Contrast
- Persuasion

The following sections will highlight the process of each essay and show steps that students should follow to improve their overall essay skills – the reader should also refer back to previous sections when reviewing paragraph set up.

1. The different types of essays

A. Descriptive

1) As with descriptive paragraphs, descriptive essays are pictures of the writers' thoughts and ideas. The main importance of writing this type of essay is to be detailed and that means spending a lot of time and effort brainstorming. The writer should be very familiar with the topic or do a lot of research; the writer should also focus on growing the details from least important to most important. The paragraphs should provide as much detail as possible and a conclusion should sum up the description – this essay will provide a picture for the reader

2) It is important during the brainstorming process that the writer develops as many adjectives as possible to describe the topic. It is always better too many adjectives that not enough. Try to build from small to large and take the reader on the devilment of the greater picture.

3) The writer should follow several steps

- Be focused and familiar with your topic

- Brainstorm your topic

- Map your details (as many as possible)

- Start from small to large

- Use plenty of adjectives

- Conclude with a summary description

4) Example outline of an essay

My Experience at the EURO 2012

It was a cold summer day when we were waiting for the plane to Kiev but we were excited. Jim, John, Marty, and I were on our way to cheer on the Irish team in Kiev at the Euro 2012 soccer tournament. It has been 16 long miserable years since the Irish team were last in the tournament but now they are back and we are like children waiting to open Christmas toys.

The plane ride was never ending it felt like because we were so wired and pumped about the games. We talked about what we were going to do when we landed and where we would go. We talked with fellow passengers about the team and the games and the atmosphere was electric on the plane. Beers were drunk and songs were sung, it felt at times like we were already at the games. Thankfully the flight attendants were ok with our boisterousbehavior and actually joined in a few times.

After we landed, we rested the night and got ready for the big game the next day. The morning of the game we arose with joyous expectations of the game. We got dressed, headed out the door and made our way to the stadium. The road to the stadium was full of fans, many wear green and white of Ireland and many wearing red and white of Poland. The fans were singing and dancing in the street and we decided to join in. Arm in arm with other fans dressed in green and white, we danced our way through the streets singing songs of history and hope. Tears were released by fans as we discussed the results of past games and terrible disappointments but this day there were tears of happiness as well –for the potential of success. Eventually we made our way to the stadium and we could hear the roar of the crowd, smell the sweat of the other fans. Excitement was growing and anticipation was increasing for the start of the game. The national anthem was played and thousands of fans held arms and sang their lungs out, the tension was growing and excitement was palpable. Then the Ref blew his whistle and the game started and there was an almighty roar as the Irish charged forward.

This is a example of an introduction and first body paragraph of a descriptive essay

5) Questions – write an essay on one of the following:

- Your first baseball game

- Your first soccer game

- Meeting your favorite athlete

B. Compare/contrast

1) The first step in this type if essay is too narrow your topic. In your everyday life there are a lot of topics that you can compare and contrast. When showing how things are similar you are comparing and when you are showing how things are different you are contrasting. In your essay it is important that you chose to either compare or contrast – it is very hard to do both and would result in a very long essay.

2) When writing a comparison essay the writer should use several contrasts between the issues you are comparing. Use transition words such as however or despite to show that you will be comparing rather than contrasting

3) When writing a contrasting essay the writer should use several comparisons between the issues you are contrasting.

4) Steps should be followed when writing this type of essay

- Narrow your topic
- Be sure to use the correct method (compare or contrast)
- Brainstorm thoroughly
- Have a detailed outline

5) Transition words are used to smoothly move from one point to the next.

- Compare
  - Similarly
  - By comparison
  - Just as
  - Likewise
  - In the same way
- Contrast
- On the other hand
- However
- Except for

- While

6) Compare – the following outline could be used when comparing the makers of football boots to evaluate quality and cost.

- Introduction
- Thesis statement
- Types of football boots
- Nike
- Adidas
- Quality
- Nike
- Adidas
- Cost
- Nike
- Adidas
- Conclusion

7) Contrast – Koreas two favorite sports

- Introduction

- thesis

- Field

- Soccer

- Baseball

- Structure

- Soccer

- Baseball

- Rules

- Soccer

- Baseball

- Conclusion

8) Example of a contrasting essay: The following is a part essay is a contrasting essay on types of cars –

> Audi and Kia
> Audi and Kia are two types of cars that people want to purchase because of the

value and status. While the cars are similar in their capabilities and service, there are many differences between them. Appearance, performance, and cost, are some of the main differences between them.

Both Audi and Kia are some of the most attractive looking cars in today's car market but from different viewpoints. Audi is a more expensive valued car and is supposedly more superior in design and technology. Experts state that it has an overall more attractive body shape and a more luxurious interior with many more perks than are necessary. Kia is significantly cheaper than Audi and meets the needs of the average consumer in the car market. It has many of the same interior perks that an Audi has but they are built with cheaper materials and therefore the cost is cheaper. The Audi is built with much more expensive materials in order to have a greater overall design and to represent a value of "expensive."

The cost of a car is also a factor in deciding which car to buy. The Audi and Kia are both priced for certain markets and are promoted as such in advertisements.

The performance is another aspect that people use in deciding which car to purchase.

In conlusion

9) Questions –write an essay on one of the following topics

- Greatest soccer player

- Greatest sports teams

- Greatest Olympic athlete

C. Persuasion

In this essay, the writer is trying to convince the reader towards a certain point of view. The writer should take a position and then support that stand with as much details as possible. The writer should express ideas that catch the reader's attention. If the writer does not believe his/her position then they will not be able to convince the reader. The writer should state as many facts as possible to support their idea.

1) Steps

- Know your topic well

- Brainstorm for ideas

- Be clear in your thesis

- Catch the reader's attention in the introduction

- Hold their attention

- Use statistics

2) Examples of topics

- Baseball should (or should) not be allowed into the Olympics

- Racism should (or should not) be punished stronger

- Hooligans should (or should not) be banned for life

- Goal line technology should (or should not) be allowed

3) Part example of a persuasion essay

Goal Line Technology

The growing number of mistakes in professional football today has been lowering the overall enjoyment for many fans and players alike. Week after week, we are seeing major mistakes that are costing teams victories and in turn ruining the overall atmosphere of the stadium because of such errors. Therefore, it is important that FIFA should introduce goal line technology as a way to limit mistakes that happen in professional football leagues and at international tournaments. By having goal line technology, FIFA can provide reassurances to fans and players that mistakes will be eliminated.

There have been numerous mistakes at all levels of football today. From the World Cup to local professional leagues, teams have been cheated out of victories and have lost games because of poor refereeing decisions. These decisions have far lasting effects on teams with promotion and relegation. Teams who are relegated lose millions of pounds/dollars and therefore it is imperative that all potential mistakes are eliminated before a ball is kicked.

Besides team issues, fans are adamant that goal line technology should be used because they want to enjoy an honest game and not one marred by mistakes. Fans go to the game to watch games and are do not mind losing to a better team but do mind losing to mistakes made by referees.

In conclusion, if FIFA install goal line technology it will prevent mistakes by referees that negatively affect both players and fans. It can only improve the overall performance of the game and maintain a sense of fairness during the game.

4) Questions - Write an essay on one of the following topics

- Goal line technology should be used in soccer

- The Government should (should not) be in control of sport

- Separate areas in stadiums should (should not) be provided for non-smokers.

- Physical contact should (should not) be removed from children's sports

- Youth coaches should (should not) have to submit a criminal background check.

2. The reading

With IBM and Motorola out, will NFL go big in tech category?

Four months after the Super Bowl and two months before training camps open, the NFL's offseason scoreboard reads thusly: two sponsors out and one renewed for the team on Park Avenue.

Longtime NFL sponsor IBM, a league sponsor since 2003, has opted not to renew its league sponsorship rights, joining Motorola (SportsBusiness Journal, March 19) as another veteran sponsor deciding not to return to the NFL. While "Big Blue" is more familiar as a nickname for the New Jersey-based Super Bowl champs, the tech industry version has been a model business-to-business sponsor during its tenure as an NFL corporate sponsor, using league infrastructure projects like the digitization of NFL Films and other IT projects to demonstrate its capabilities.

Without sharing considerable detail on the non-renewal, Rick Singer, who heads IBM's sponsorships as vice president of client executive marketing, called it an amicable split.

The headset rights held by Motorola could be packaged as part of a broader category.

"It was a good nine-year run," he said. "We had some very good discussions, but we decided that the things they want to do aren't the same as what we want to. It wasn't about money as much as it was about each party's philosophy on the [technology] category."

Singer said no decision has been made yet on whether the healthy IBM budget line that was used to support NFL rights will be re-allocated to another sports sponsorship, here or abroad. IBM's domestic sponsorship portfolio includes tennis' U.S. Open, The Masters, the USGA and the Tony Awards.

As for the NFL rationale in all things tech, we're told that the league is on the street with the framework of a larger technology deal, and that the thought within league circles is that adding IBM's broad category rights in computer hardware, software and IT services to those formerly held by departed telecom hardware rights holder Motorola could form the rudiments of a broad technology deal. Such a sponsorship could include Motorola-like headset branding, integration of tablet PCs on NFL sidelines, widespread use of tablets by coaches and as playbooks, and rewiring NFL stadiums.

Since it would involve the league's competition committee and league and team marketing and sponsorship teams working together, the politics of such a deal are complex enough to render it nearly impossible. As in all cases, however, the NFL's magnitude will allow it to set the bar, both in rights fees and scope, in whatever tech deal it achieves.

We do not expect tablet market leader Apple to pay rights fees to any sports property any time soon. We do believe that any secondary brand, be it Lenovo (an IBM stepchild, for those in search of potential irony) or Samsung, could use the power of the NFL to quickly make a credible claim at being the No. 2 brand to Apple.

Madonna's Super Bowl halftime show will be the last for Bridgestone.

Hard to believe the NFL will be able to fashion such a complex deal in time for the coming season. Looking at it through the lens of Motorola's lapsed telecom deal, club marketers have already been told that while the league does not expect to have a telecom hardware deal before the coming season, the category is still off limits for clubs to sell.

What will the coaches' headsets, which have carried branding since the mid-1990s, look like next season? We're told that without a sponsor, that valuable real estate would promote NFL.com or NFL Network. However, we're also cautioned that the category is changing week to week, so stay tuned, via whatever handheld device you deem most appropriate.

TIRE-D OF THE SHOW?: Well-placed NFL sources tell us that Bridgestone has extended its NFL deal, but opted out of its title sponsorship of the Super Bowl halftime show. Bridgestone's last sponsorship agreement bound it to the NFL through the 2014 season, and it had titled the halftime extravaganza since 2008, during which musicians Tom Petty, Bruce Springsteen, The Who, the Black Eyed Peas and Madonna have headlined.

Bridgestone is shifting its NFL efforts to a "year-round platform, including training camp, kickoff, and will still have a presence at Super Bowl," we're told by one involved marketer.

In winning Sponsor of the Year accolades at the Sports Business Awards recently, Bridgestone marketers cited their affiliation with jewel events of the biggest sports properties as the key strategy in growing both brand equity and sales measures in what has been a declining tire market. However, Madonna's performance at this year's Super Bowl halftime show included rapper M.I.A. flipping the bird. M.I.A.'s childish action was seen by a record television audience of 111.3 million viewers. So we're wondering if that played a role in the tire brand veering right with its NFL rights.

That puts the NFL back on the street with its Super Bowl halftime show for the first time under its current marketing and sales regime. Another rhetorical question before departing: Would that inventory be enough to attract a tech sponsor of the type outlined above?

A. QUESTIONS

1) How has technology influenced sponsorship?

2) Has technology improved the NFL or its marketing strategies?

3) Do you think that having technology so ingrained in the NFL diminishes the actual focus on the game?

3. Writing assignment.

A. Write an essay on a topic of your choice and use one of the following techniques

1) Opinion

2) Persuasion

3) Compare/contrast

4) description

‹‹‹ MEMO ›››

‹‹‹ MEMO ›››

<<< MEMO >>>

‹‹‹ MEMO ›››

Let's learn English Through Sport
WRITING!

Chapter 8

Business Writing

Chapter 8

Business Writing

In this chapter, reader will learn what is important within business communication. The authors will show the correct way to communicate via email, cover letter and resume, letter writing and thank you notes

1. Email Communication

While Email has become the quickest way to contact others, it is an avenue that is often abused because of a person's misunderstanding of how they should write. Many times people are often too formal or too informal; therefore it is important to find a middle ground.

A. What to put in an email

1) Have a clear subject line

2) Make it short and concise

3) Make sure that your email is addressed to a specific person

4) Address the person as Mr./Mrs./Dr. until they inform you to call them something more informal

5) Be careful of a lack of punctuation

6) Do not use derogatory or informal language

7) Write your email using business language and not as you would speak to friends

8) Include your contact information at the end of the email

9) Only include attachments when asked to send them

B. What not to include

1) Do not include text speak - the flowing are only a few examples but when writing an email you should use language and terminology that you would normally write in a letter.

- IDK – I don't know

- 2 – to

- 4 – for

- LMBO – laughing my butt off

2) Do not include vulgar jokes – nobody appreciates them and they can cause serious problems for your organization.

3) Do not put your email all in CAPS.

4) Do not use crazy lettering or color schemes

5) Have an appropriate email handle

- Hotguy2675 or sexygirl343@hotmail.com are not appropriate

6) Have a clear background on your email

7) Examples of emails: Poor Email:

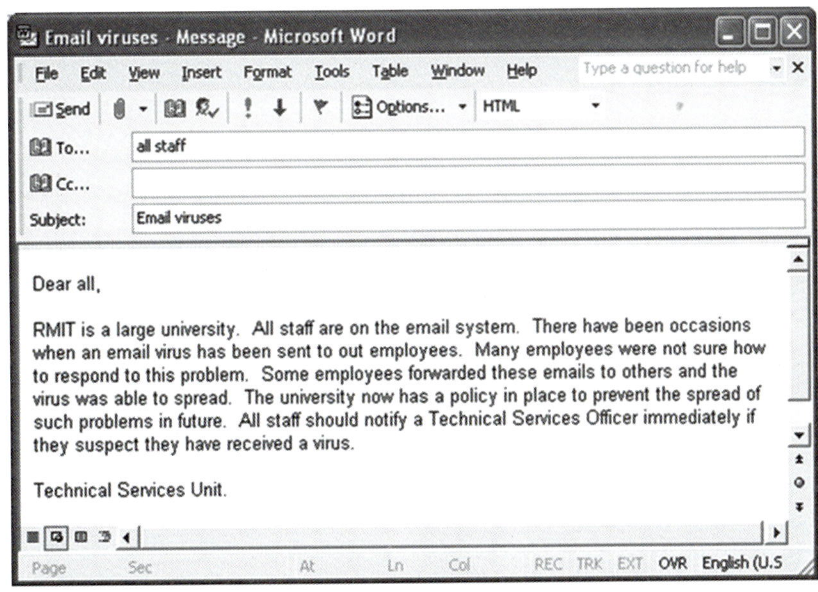

Email viruses - Message - Microsoft Word

File Edit View Insert Format Tools Table Window Help

To... all staff

Cc...

Subject: Email viruses

Dear all,

RMIT is a large university. All staff are on the email system. There have been occasions when an email virus has been sent to out employees. Many employees were not sure how to respond to this problem. Some employees forwarded these emails to others and the virus was able to spread. The university now has a policy in place to prevent the spread of such problems in future. All staff should notify a Technical Services Officer immediately if they suspect they have received a virus.

Technical Services Unit.

- The email does not have any contact information except for the email address

- The subject line is very vague

- Too much unnecessary information

8) Examples of emails: Good Email:

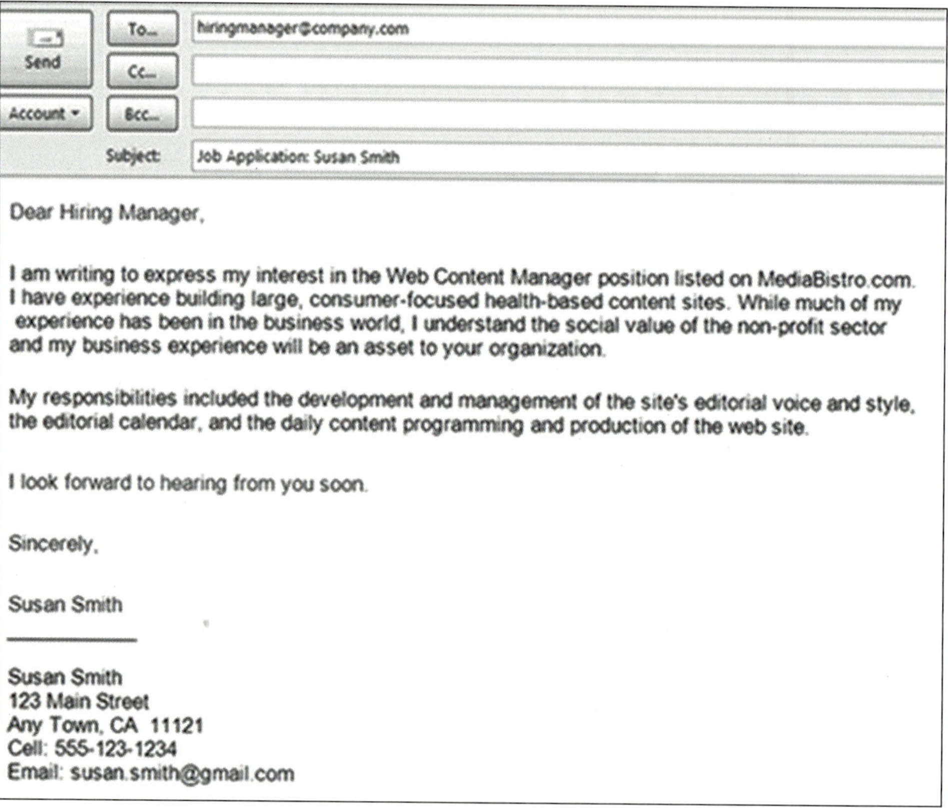

To... hiringmanager@company.com

Cc...

Bcc...

Subject: Job Application: Susan Smith

Dear Hiring Manager,

I am writing to express my interest in the Web Content Manager position listed on MediaBistro.com. I have experience building large, consumer-focused health-based content sites. While much of my experience has been in the business world, I understand the social value of the non-profit sector and my business experience will be an asset to your organization.

My responsibilities included the development and management of the site's editorial voice and style, the editorial calendar, and the daily content programming and production of the web site.

I look forward to hearing from you soon.

Sincerely,

Susan Smith

Susan Smith
123 Main Street
Any Town, CA 11121
Cell: 555-123-1234
Email: susan.smith@gmail.com

- Good language

- Addressed properly

- Contact information

- Clear and concise

- Good information

The purpose of a resume is to market yourself to obtain a future job. The resume will highlight your experiences and strengths to prospective employers. It is the first impression that you will give to an employer so make sure that it is correct!!!!

A. What is a resume

1) Marketing tool – showcase your positives

2) Summary of your experience

3) Future capabilities

B. What to include in a resume

1) Identity

- Contact Information: Name, address, phone number, email address – make sure that all are current and working

- Objective – Explains what you are looking for and is specific to each job.

- Should be short and concise

2) Educational background

- University Information: Name, Degree, GPA, and year of graduation

- High School information is optional

3) Experience

- Should start with your most recent experience first

- Relevant

- Work based and Educational based

- Show an employer you have acquired experience

- Related

- Could be applied to your future capabilities

4) Activities

- Club and organization memberships

- Volunteer work

5) Achievements (optional)

6) Skills

- You should put down relevant skills such as computer based skills, language skills, or leadership skills. For example:

- Microsoft Word

- Adobe

- Apple

- French, German, Korean

7) References

- It is important that your references are aware that you are piutting them in your resume. Therefore, get there approval first.

- Two ways for references

- One - put names, addresses, phone numbers, and email addresses in the actual resume

- Two – state that references will be "available upon request"– this means that if any potential employer is interested, then they can contact the references if necessary.

C. What to do in a resume

1) Be focused

2) Use strong action words (see list at the end of the chapter)

3) Make it easy to read

4) Use facts and not opinions

D. What not to do in a resume

1) Avoid Personal information–Height, weight etc.

2) Health Issues

3) DO NOT LIE OR EXXAGERATE

4) Do not be sloppy – check your wording and spelling

5) Hold a grudge against other people (former employers)

D. Example of a good resume

Name

Permanent Address

487 London Ave.

London, UKBT16 7852

(010) XXXX-XXXX

jimjames@gmail.com

Education:

Bachelors June2012

Major: Accountancy Management

London School of Business

Overall GPA: 4.4/5.0 Major GPA: 4.75.0

Related Experience:

McDonnell's Accountants, Fulham, London October 2009-Present

Accounts Assistant Manager

- Perform duties between employees.
- Oversee the management of old accounts.
- Prepare and conduct intern training.
- Evaluate intern evaluations.
- Performed maintenance and repairs on computers.
- Coordinated schedules for interns.
- Maintained inventory of supplies.
- Coordinated meeting schedules for employees.

Student Council

- Assisted students with problems.
- Maintained communication between teachers and students.

Other Experience:

Intern, M.E.L. Gormley&Gormely CPA, London

Intern Nat West Bank, Fulham, London

Sales Associate, TESCO, Fulham, London

Activities:

Association of Student Account Professionals

Skills:

Fluent in German, French, and English Internet

Microsoft office, adobe, SPSS, Web page creator

The above resume is:

- Readable
- Has relevant information listed first and easy to find
- Action Verbs used
- One page
- Recent graduate and the Education section is listed first

3. Cover letters

A. What is a cover letter

The purpose of a cover letter is to introduce yourself along with your resume to any prospective employer. To request an interview or show interest in a particular job and shows them your potential writing and communication skills.

B. How to write a cover letter

The cover letter emphasizes additional skills, experiences, or abilities not found in a resume and expand on experience in resume or include experience not in resumes.

C. Two Types of letters

1) One – Letter of application

- Targets identified positions

- Tailor the contents of this letter to the job description or employer

2) Two – Letter of inquiry

- Used to inquire about potential jobs

- Used as a networking letter

D. Three parts to a letter

1) Introduction (1 paragraph)

- Say who you are and what you want

- Name the position that you are applying for and how you heard about it

- Spark the interest of the reader

2) Body (1-2 paragraphs)

- Stress your strongest points / qualifications

- Expand on points in your resume

- Emphasize why you should be hired

3) Conclusion (1 paragraph)

- Thank the person for reading your information

- Ask for an interview

- Provide your information for a follow up

D. Examples

Morgan A. Maxwell

626 East Second Street, Bloomington, IN 47404 812/555-0000
23 Maxwell Lane, Morgan, MI 49423 616/555-3333

April 16, 2004

Hillary Hirer
Director of Human Resources
Acme Public Relations
1 Paycheck Avenue
Chicago, IL 60111

Dear Ms. Hirer:

The importance of communication, leadership, and problem solving in the public relations field prompts me to respond to your recent vacancy announcement for a Marketing and Special Events Coordinator. I became aware of the position while exploring the job listings through the Indiana University Arts and Sciences Placement Office. Acme is a leader in working with the public sector, which is why I am particularly interested in your company.

At ESPN Television, I had the opportunity to work with a wide variety of people as a media relations intern. I coordinated press conferences and interviews with athletic teams and assisted with daily events and shows for ESPN broadcasts. These tasks required a high level of verbal communication skills, attention to detail, and the ability to interact with a diverse range of people. Through the Semester at Sea Program, I had the opportunity to live, study, and work in different cultures. I believe my experience meets the position requirement that an individual be comfortable with a wide range of audiences.

The public relations sector requires strong leadership skills. As the Student Director for the campus tour guide team, I was responsible for coordinating over 25 tours weekly and for facilitating meetings for 65 student tour guides. This experience enhanced my leadership and motivational abilities. In addition, membership in the Alpha Alpha Alpha Sorority provided many opportunities to gain valuable leadership skills.

I believe my education, work experience and leadership abilities make me a strong candidate for the Marketing and Special Events Coordinator position. Enclosed is my resume that further outlines my education and work experience. I am excited to learn more about Acme Public Relations and look forward to the opportunity to discuss this position with you in person. Thank you for your time and consideration and I look forward to meeting with you soon.

Sincerely,

Morgan Maxwell

Enclosure

Chase B. Kappel

523 Sandstone Drive • Bloomington, IN 47404 • (812) 555-5555
11543 Tulip Street • Indianapolis, IN 46023 • (317) 444-4444
chasekappel@indiana.edu

April 17, 2004

Ms. Hillary Hirer
Director of Human Resources
Acme Public Relations
1 Paycheck Avenue
Chicago, IL 60111

Dear Ms. Hirer:

I have spent the past year exploring career options that would allow me the opportunity to apply skills I enjoy most and feel are my strongest attributes. The ability to communicate effectively in writing, to analyze difficult situations and suggest strategic solutions, and to lead others from planning stages to execution are the traits that have drawn me to the public relations sector. As my research continued, I was drawn to your organization in particular because of the work you do with the public sector. I was excited to find through the Indiana University Arts and Sciences Placement Office that you currently have a position open as a Marketing and Special Events Coordinator.

As a recreation intern at the Fishers Parks and Recreation Department, I had the opportunity to hone my planning skills. I created and implemented a weekly "Music Under the Stars" evening. This program required a high level of organization and attention to detail, along with effective marketing strategies and clear communication with city officials and local media. As a result of the program's success, it will be continued this year.

In addition to classroom knowledge and relevant work experiences, I have participated in extracurricular activities where I had the opportunity to develop many important skills. As the Assistant Director of Forums for Union Board, I worked within a committee to select program topics and then carry out or delegate tasks. This role made me into an effective team member who can lead brainstorming sessions and direct conversation flow. I also developed the ability to analyze the target market and choose promotional tactics to most efficiently reach the target demographic.

Enclosed you will find my resume which further outlines my educational background and experiences. I would like the opportunity to meet with you in person to discuss the Marketing and Special Events Coordinator position. I will contact you on Monday, April 30th to ensure the arrival of my materials and inquire about scheduling an interview or you may reach me at 812/555-5555 or chasekappel@indiana.edu. Thank you for your time and consideration and I look forward to talking with you soon.

Sincerely,

Chase B. Kappel

Enclosure

4. Thank you notes

A. What is a thank you note?

A thank you note is a card or note that you send to a prospective employer after an interview or meeting that can reaffirm your interest in a position.

B. Why you should write one

- Reiterate your interest

- Reemphasis your strengths

C. How to write a thank you note

- Send within 24-48 hours after an interview

- Keep it professional and easy to read

- Proofread and have no errors

- Only email if this is your mode of communication

D. Example

SAMPLE THANK YOU LETTER

178 Green Street
Kingston, MA 02364
September 24, 2002

Pat Cummings
Editor
Any Publishing Company
1140 Main Street
Boston, MA 02106

Dear Mr. Cummings:

I want to thank you for interviewing me for the Editorial Assistant position yesterday at the Indiana University Career Development Center . I enjoyed meeting you and learning more about the Any Publishing Company and your work on the *Internet Primer.*

This position offers an incredible opportunity to learn about the entire editorial and production processes involved in creating a book. I believe my education as well as my written and editorial skills developed as an Editor with the *Indiana Daily Student* fit ideally with the job requirements outlined. Above all, I am very eager to learn, and I know that I could make a significant contribution to the project.

I would like to express my strong interest in the position and in working with you and Daniel Connelly. This is the ideal opportunity I seek. Please feel free to call me at (617) 555-5555 or contact me at chris_smith@someuniversity.edu if I can provide you with any additional information.

Again, thank you for the interview and your consideration. I look forward to hearing from you soon.

Sincerely,

Chris Smith

Chris Smith

5. List of Action Words for Resumes

accelerated	assured	combined	credited
accomplished	attended	commented	critiqued
accounted for	audited	communicated	cut
achieved	authored	compared	debated
acquired	authorized	compiled	dealt
added	awarded	completed	DECIDED
addressed	began	composed	defined
adjusted	bolstered	computed	delegated
ADMINISTERED	boosted	conceived	delivered
ADVISED	bought	conceptualized	demonstrated
aided	briefed	concluded	described
allocated	brought	conditioned	designed
alphabetized	budgeted	conducted	determined
ANALYZED	built	considered	DEVELOPED
answered	canceled	constructed	devised
anticipated	calculated	consulted	diagnosed
appeared	cataloged	continued	did
applied	caught	contracted	digested
appointed	caused	controlled	diminished
appraised	chaired	converted	DIRECTED
approved	changed	convinced	discovered
arbitrated	checked	COORDINATED	discussed
argued	chopped	copied	distributed
arranged	chose	corrected	documented
assessed	classified	counseled	drafted
assigned	cleared up	counted	dramatized
assisted	closed	crafted	drew up
assumed	collected	created	dropped

earned	financed	influenced	mediated
EDITED	focused	innovated	met
educated	forecast	inspected	modified
elected	foresaw	installed	monitored
eliminated	FORMULATED	instructed	motivated
employed	forwarded	insured	moved
encouraged	fostered	interpreted	named
endorsed	found	interviewed	NEGOTIATED
enjoyed	gathered	INTRODUCED	netted
enlarged	gave	investigated	observed
enlisted	grabbed	involved	opened
ensured	graded	issued	operated
entered	granted	joined	ordered
ESTABLISHED	greeted	kept	ORGANIZED
estimated	grossed	labored	overcame
EVALUATED	hastened	launched	oversaw
examined	heightened	learned	paid
excelled	helped	leased	painted
executed	highlighted	lectured	participated
exercised	hiked	led	perceived
expanded	housed	licensed	performed
expedited	hunted	listed	PERSUADED
experienced	identified	located	pioneered
experimented	IMPLEMENTED	logged	placed
explained	improved	made	PLANNED
explored	included	maintained	played
expressed	incorporated	MANAGED	policed
extended	increased	mapped	prepared
familiarized	indexed	matched	presented
filed	indicated	maximized	prevailed
filled	INITIATED	measured	processed

procured	represented	specified	translated
produced	researched	spoke	transported
profited	rescued	started	traveled
programmed	responded	stated	treated
prohibited	resulted in	stopped	turned
projected	returned	straightened	tutored
promoted	revamped	streamlined	typed
proofed	revealed	strengthened	uncovered
proposed	reviewed	stripped	unearthed
proved	revised	studied	unfurled
provided	saved	SUBMITTED	updated
published	saw	substituted	upped
purchased	scheduled	suggested	used
pursued	scouted	summarized	visited
put	screened	SUPERVISED	welcomed
qualified	scrutinized	supported	won
quickened	selected	surmounted	worked
ran	sent	surveyed	
ranked	served	tackled	
rated	serviced	targeted	
realized	set	taught	
received	shipped	tested	
recognized	shored up	tightened	
reconciled	showed	took	
recruited	sifted	took over	
reduced	simplified	totaled	
regulated	smoothed	toured	
renovated	SOLVED	tracked	
replaced	sorted	trained	
replied	sought	transferred	
reported	spearheaded	transformed	

<<< **MEMO** >>>

‹‹‹ MEMO ›››

First printed | August 20, 2012.
First published | August 30, 2012.
The writer | Joe Trolan Ph.D Candidate & Seong-Hee Park Ph.D
The publisher | Park, Chul
Hankuk University of Foreign Studies Press Center
107 Imun-ro Dongdaemun-gu, Seoul, 130-791
Tel : 82-2-2173-2495/7
Fax : 82-2-2173-3363
Homepage : http://press.hufs.ac.kr
e-mail : press@hufs.ac.kr
Registration of publisher | 6-6(April 30, 1969)

ISBN 978-89-7464-753-7 13740 ₩15,000